CITIES OF THE BIBLICAL WO

Excavation in Palestine

Roger Moorey

Senior Assistant Keeper, Department of Antiquities,
Ashmolean Museum, Oxford

LUTTERWORTH PRESS
CAMBRIDGE

CITIES OF THE BIBLICAL WORLD

General Editor:
Graham I. Davies, Lecturer in Divinity,
  Cambridge University.

Other Titles:
Qumran, Philip R. Davies, Lecturer in Biblical Studies,
  University of Sheffield.
Jericho, John R. Bartlett, Lecturer in Divinity, and Fellow of
  Trinity College, Dublin.
Megiddo, Graham I. Davies.
Ugarit (Ras Shamra), Adrian H. W. Curtis, Lecturer in Old
  Testament Studies, University of Manchester.

First published in 1981
Reprinted, 1988

ISBN 0–7188–2432–6

Printed and bound in Great Britain

Contents

List of Illustrations

Preface

Books on the archaeology of Palestine and adjacent regions commonly take for granted a knowledge of the aims and methods of archaeology as an intellectual discipline, whilst general books on these topics, if they refer to this region at all, are likely to do so in derogatory terms. One of the most vivid and influential books on archaeological method, the late Sir Mortimer Wheeler's *Archaeology from the Earth* (1954), took many of its most cogent illustrations of how *not* to excavate from the history of archaeological research in Palestine. The reputation of archaeology there has been further compromised among scholars at large by the abuse of archaeological evidence in popular and widely read books seeking with its aid to demonstrate the 'truth' of the Bible: a matter of theology not of archaeology. Although influential and powerful voices have been raised in recent years to demonstrate the fallacy of this approach, its shadow is long and pervasive, obscuring much good work.

This book is neither an apology for obvious faults nor a manual of archaeological techniques in Palestine. It is designed as a simple introduction for all those people with little or no archaeological knowledge, not least among them biblical students who are interested in the archaeology of Palestine. I have assumed that they have never been on a Near Eastern excavation, indeed may never have the opportunity to do so, yet wish to know how the evidence they seek is gained and processed. It is largely restricted, by the terms of reference of the series to which it belongs, to the period from about 2000 BC to the Roman Empire. It deals therefore with text aided or historic archaeology, not with prehistory, the field in which the contribution of archaeology to the study of human society is pre-eminent. Many problems and techniques are shared, but historic archaeology has generally received less attention than prehistoric, often to the extent that many laymen regard the terms 'archaeology' and 'prehistory' as synonymous.

I have used notes as sparingly as possible, usually only to give the source of quotations or of the specific archaeological examples mentioned in the text. These I have quite intentionally drawn from a relatively restricted range of sites: those whose publication is full, reasonably accessible, and most readily intelligible to a non-specialist reader. The reading of archaeological reports is a skill only to be learnt by practice, which should not be inhibited at the outset by encounters with the more intractable examples of the genre. The lists of recommended reading are designed to direct the reader to the most appropriate treatments of subjects only cursorily mentioned here.

It is not always easy to know how best to advise the newcomer to approach a subject after a general introduction (chapter 1), whether through a summary of its historical development (chapter 2), or through a brief review of how things are now done (chapter 3). I have decided to place history before procedures; but many readers may prefer to read chapter 3 after 1 and then turn back to 2. They are written, I hope, so that either the direct or the indirect approach is possible.

Acknowledgements

I am most grateful to Dr. Graham Davies, the editor of this series, for his comments on the manuscript, and to Dr. Sebastian Brock for advice on specific points; for what remains I alone am responsible. My thanks are also due to Mrs. Ruth Amiran and Dr. Aharon Kempinski for help in obtaining photographs, and to Mrs. Pat Clarke for making the drawings.

For permission to reproduce photographs here I am indebted to the directors, or their deputies, of the Tel Arad, Tel Masos and Tel Beersheba expeditions; to the British School of Archaeology in Jerusalem; to the Israel Department of Antiquities and Museums; to Professor J. D. Muhly; to the Trustees of the British Museum; to the Visitors of the Ashmolean Museum, Oxford; to Mrs C. M. Bennett and Dr. G. Davies.

Abbreviations

A.A.S.O.R.	*Annual of the American Schools of Oriental Research*, New Haven.
B.A.S.O.R.	*Bulletin of the American Schools of Oriental Research*, New Haven.
Bib. Arch.	*The Biblical Archaeologist*, New Haven
Encyclopedia	M. Avi-Yonah (Ed.), *Encyclopedia of Archaeological Excavations in the Holy Land*, I-IV, Oxford.
I.E.J.	*Israel Exploration Journal*, Jerusalem.
P.E.Q.	*Palestine Exploration Quarterly*, London.
Q.D.A.J.	*Quarterly of the Department of Antiquities of Jordan*, Amman.
Q.D.A.P.	*Quarterly of the Department of Antiquities of Palestine*, Jerusalem.
Z.D.P.V.	*Zeitschrift des Deutschen Palästina – Vereins*, Wiesbaden.

Chronological Table

Egypt		Palestine		Mesopotamia
	AD		AD	
Roman Empire		Roman Empire		Parthians
	BC		BC	
	30		140	
Hellenistic Period		Hellenistic Period		Hellenistic Period
(Ptolemaic Dynasty)		(Seleucid and local		(Seleucids)
		dynasts)		
	330		330	
←		Achaemenid Persian		→
(Intermittently)		Empire		
	500		500	
		Babylonian Captivity		
		Iron Age IIB-C		Neo-Babylonian Period
		(Divided Monarchy)		
The Late Period				Neo-Assyrian Period
		Iron Age IIA		Middle Assyrian Period
	1000	(United Monarchy)	1000	Middle Babylonian
		Iron Age I		Period
The New Kingdom		Late Bronze Age II		The Kassite Period
	1500	Late Bronze Age I	1500	
The Second		Middle Bronze Age II		The Old Babylonian
Intermediate		(IIB-C)		Period
The Middle Kingdom				
		Middle Bronze Age I		The Isin-Larsa Period
	2000	(IIA)	2000	
The First Intermediate		Intermediate Period		The Ur III Period
		(Early Bronze IV –		
		Middle Bronze I)		The Akkadian Period
The Old Kingdom		Early Bronze Age III		Early Dynastic III
	2500		2500	
		Early Bronze Age II		Early Dynastic II
				Early Dynastic I
Proto-Dynastic	3000		3000	
		Early Bronze Age I		The Jamdat Nasr
				Period
		Proto-Urban Period		
				The Uruk Period
Pre-Dynastic		The Chalcolithic Period		
	4000		4000	The Ubaid Period

1

Introducing Archaeology

As a favourite of the mass media for over a quarter of a century archaeology would appear not to be in need of an introduction; but it is a very special image of the subject which in that time has most often been offered to the public. This study of man in the past, through all the confused and scattered debris which his activities have left to be recovered by the spade, is commonly presented in one of two ways. If both are equally misleading, for they over-emphasise one aspect at the expense of others, both are instructive indications of what most laymen are likely to know and appreciate in archaeology. First and foremost emphasis is laid on discovery; not, unfortunately, on carefully pursued programmes of research extending over years, but much more often on the sensational and unexpected discoveries, described in isolation from their proper context in the evolution of archaeological enquiry. It is implied, if not actually stated, that the chief goal of archaeology is 'the firstest with the mostest,' to borrow an American scholar's memorable phrase.[1]

A second theme is no less pervasive. This represents the archaeologist above all as a master craftsman recovering from the earth, with an ever more impressive range of scientific aids, the treasures of the past. Such indeed he may be, but if he did no more than this he would be indulging in an arid antiquarianism more reminiscent of the 1880s than of the 1980s. For modern archaeologists interpretation and evaluation of evidence, the reconstruction of ancient societies in the widest possible sense, is the primary aim. Advanced archaeological theorists would now go further and see its ultimate goals in generalisations about the nature of culture, in the anthropological sense, and even of human social behaviour.

The emergence of archaeology as an independent subject in modern times was assisted by accumulating evidence from geological sources for the association of man-made stone tools and extinct fauna, attributable to 'a very remote period indeed, even beyond that of the present world' (John Frere, 1797). For years theological objections to such a view crippled its growth. Not until about 1860 was the existence of prehistoric man firmly established. In the meantime archaeology had adopted from geology the two basic working concepts of stratigraphy and type-fossils. *Stratigraphy* is the foundation of archaeological as well as geological chronology. It assumes that in the excavation of any sequence of undisturbed deposits, whether of natural or of man-made debris, the oldest layers are to be found at the bottom and the most recent at the top. Those specific fossil animals, fishes or plants which are distinctive of particular layers in a geological sequence are known to geologists as *type-fossils*. In the same way the archaeologist isolates as his type-fossils those artefacts which characterise successive levels of occupational debris in a particular settlement and studies their changes across time and space (typology).

As archaeological exploration proceeded through survey and excavation, certain objects were seen to occur in one locality in the same general order of succession as similar objects in other localities. The archaeologist then inferred, as did the geologist, that such assemblages of similar artefacts were contemporary. With the help of such type-fossils it was thus possible to define overall periods in the archaeological sequence. The result, combining studies of stratigraphy and typology, was only a relative chronology in which a period or an object was positioned in relation to others, but not precisely in a succession of years reckoned from the Christian era. To achieve an *absolute chronology* in years BC/AD, and only through such a firm framework of time may causes and effects be properly judged, the relative archaeological sequence had to be pinned down. This was done either by cross-dating to a region with a historical chronology established from texts and astronomical observations (see pp. 74ff.) or by using an independent scientific method for establishing absolute dates, such as Carbon-14 (see pp. 77ff.). Even then, for the pre-classical world, absolute chronologies have margins of error far greater than those familiar to modern historians. Rare indeed are single dates which may confidently be cited as one might 1066, 1588 or 1914; more often possible margins of error running into decades or generations have to be taken into account.

Time, if a fundamental dimension in creating the framework for an archaeology of any area, is not the only or indeed the main one with which the excavator is concerned. He must classify his finds for interpretation in terms of human activity, of social and economic life. Much of the time he constructs models or patterns (not always consciously) of the past to give coherence and meaning to the data available to him at any one time. He then modifies or reformulates his models as new evidence or new ways of thinking render them obsolete. The oldest, and still for many regions, the primary classification of this kind is a simple technological one evolved first to classify museum collections and then confirmed by excavation in Denmark in the first half of the last century. This *Three-Age system*, was constructed in the

Plate 1　Water-colour of Jericho by J. M. W. Turner, after a sketch by the Rev. R. Masters, engraved on steel by W. Finden as plate 4 of volume II of *The Biblical Keepsake* (1835).

belief that men had once used only stone for tools and weapons, then stone and bronze (an alloy of copper and tin), and still later also iron. Regularly modified and refined, this chronological scheme of Stone, Bronze and Iron still provides the primary archaeological classification for Palestine (see pp. 68f.).

A third strand in the early history of archaeology, apart from the geological and technological, linked this new study of man in antiquity to *ethnography*: the descriptive study of modern primitive peoples. In 1859 when Darwin finally published his theory of evolution he expressed no view about its effect on the problem of man's ancestry, but his work certainly made people more prepared to accept the great antiquity of man by then evident from contemporary geological researches. It was T. H. Huxley who rapidly turned Darwinian theories to the study of man, with profound long-term implications for archaeology. Put in its crudest terms it encouraged the search for evidence to show how man had evolved from a maker of simple stone tools to a nineteenth century gunsmith. Moreover, the newly fashionable biological evolution, assumed to be universal and progressive, provided the pattern for

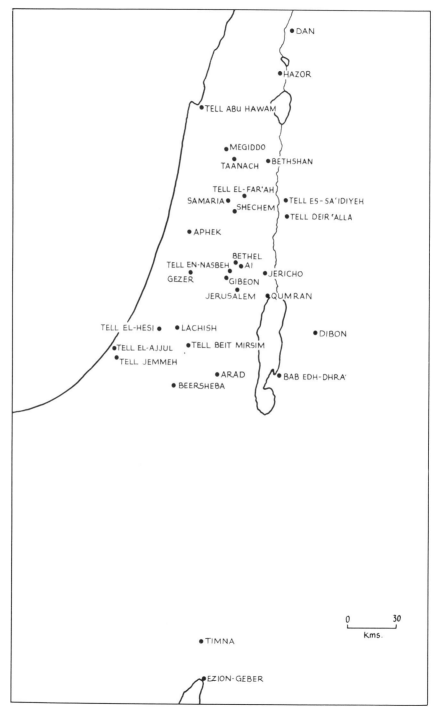

Figure 1 Map of Palestine to show the main sites mentioned in the text.

study of cultural evolution. Now, it was argued, ancient societies might appropriately be understood by analogy with those contemporary primitive societies held to be at a comparable stage of development; or, as Morlot put it explicitly in 1861, 'Ethnography is, consequently to archaeology what physical geography is to geology, namely: a thread of induction in the labyrinth of the past, and a starting point into those comparative researches of which the end is the knowledge of mankind, and its development through successive generations.'[2] Although it has ebbed and flowed in significance, this relationship endures. Argument by ethnographical analogy has in recent years returned to favour among archaeologists, albeit in forms different from those fashionable fifty or a hundred years ago.

This approach is well illustrated in the area where archaeology and biblical studies overlap by recent attempts to use ethnographical and anthropological hypotheses, drawn from the study of modern nomadic populations in the Near East, to understand comparable phenomena in the Old Testament, particularly in the Patriarchal narratives.[3] These studies have been greatly assisted by the large archive of tablets from the royal palace, of the eighteenth century BC, at Mari on the middle Euphrates in Syria. Royal officials in this great urban centre were in regular and direct contact with the tribes of the Syrian desert to the west of the city. Their records provide a remarkable documentation of the relationship between tribal societies, embracing both settled villagers and semi-nomadic pastoralists, and aggressive and powerful city-states, which was a recurrent theme in ancient Near Eastern history. The ethnographical analogies may not wholly explain the textual and archaeological data available to describe an ancient situation in a particular place at a certain time, but they make the modern investigator, commonly from an urban background in the western world, aware of the full range of possibilities in a social situation wholly alien to him. The wider the range of an archaeologist's knowledge of human societies, the more open his mind, and the sharper his control in using such knowledge for comparative purposes, the more cogent and sensitive will be his explanations of the inarticulate data retrieved by survey and excavation.

Archaeological research does not have to proceed very far before the limitations of the Three-Age system, and simplistic ethnographical parallels for the full interpretation of archaeological information in human terms, are apparent. A much more flexible unit of classification conceived on a smaller scale was provided by the *archaeological culture*, which received its classic definition from Gordon Childe in 1929, 'We find certain types of remains – pots, implements, ornaments, burial rites, house forms – constantly re-curring together. We assume that such a complex is the material expression of what today would be called a people.'[4] On this assumption sites were grouped together to form 'cultures' with more attention paid to their geographical and chronological relationships and the traits characterising them than to their internal organisation. Consequently changes were more often interpreted in terms of migration and diffusion than of factors operating within any group of communities.

Although the main concern of this book is with a period when archaeological research may be related to an independent historical framework reconstructed from textual evidence, the archaeological culture remains very relevant to the study of ancient Palestine. This will be clear from any reading of such standard textbooks as Albright's *The Archaeology of Palestine* or Kathleen Kenyon's *Archaeology in the Holy Land*, or the archaeological chapters of the revised *Cambridge Ancient History*. Even if they are not explicitly used after 3000 BC many of the assumptions implicit in the idea of an archaeological culture as expressed by Childe, are present in the interpretations of archaeological material from historic periods.

Two of these assumptions are now the subject of debate; the first is a relatively technical problem for working archaeologists, but the second must concern anyone reading archaeological literature. First, it is asked, does the archaeological record contain homogeneous groups of objects (or cultures) which may in practice be distinguished as such from other groups? Second, if we accept that this is possible, are they really the material expression of a social group or people? The debate is likely to run on for years if only because the culture remains for the moment an irreplaceable piece of archaeological jargon or shorthand. So long as it is regarded as no more than a category of classification, whose interpretation in social terms must always be carefully argued and justified, it serves a useful purpose in organising the raw material from excavations.

It is when the archaeologist proceeds to write his full, longhand narrative using cultures for his basic framework, or to blend inferences from archaeological evidence into a ready made historical scheme, that he is at his most vulnerable. Where the limits of inference from *archaeological material* are to be set is a fundamental problem, still much discussed. The traditional school of thought has been admirably and clearly represented by Piggott in recent years on a number of occasions. ' . . . The nature of the archaeological evidence or of other evidence about the past, conditions and limits the nature of the information it can provide. . . . The archaeologist's view of the past is inevitably a technological and materialistic one, simply because it is based on the products of ancient technology and not because this viewpoint has any intrinsic validity. This viewpoint can be extended to cover the field of subsistence-economics by cooperation with the natural sciences . . . but beyond this point inference from archaeological evidence alone can inform

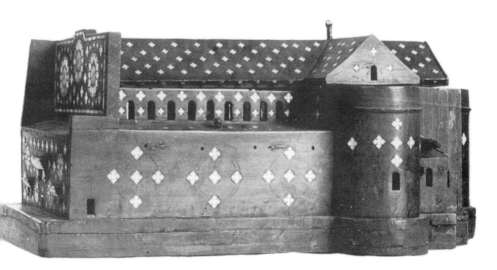

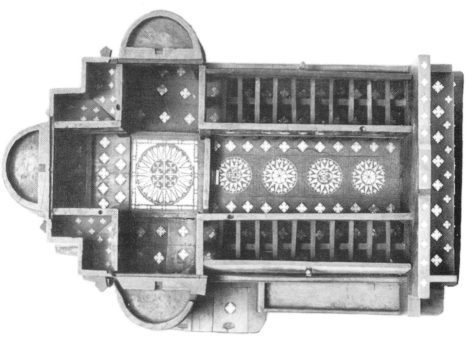

Plate 2   Two views of a wood and mother-of-pearl model of the Church of the
          Nativity of Bethlehem; seventeenth century AD. Such models of the holy
          places in Palestine are among the oldest surviving souvenirs of the great
          age of pilgrimage, produced at a time when the earliest scientific research
          into the antiquities of Palestine was beginning.

us of only the broadest aspects of social structure or religious belief, and that often in a very tentative way.'[5] For most of the readers of this book, reared in the tradition of biblical scholarship where the historical approach is taken for granted, this statement will probably seem unexceptional.

This would not be so among the advocates of the popularly named 'New Archaeology'. This was nurtured in North America, where the social sciences, in marked contrast to the European tradition, have long been anti-historical. There archaeology is regarded, with such subjects as social and physical anthropology and ethnology, as part of a broader discipline simply called 'anthropology'. It is not then surprising that the orthodox European view, expressed by Piggott, is challenged as unduly pessimistic. It is claimed that the limitations are not in the evidence itself, but in the methodologies by which the archaeologist has until now processed it. Archaeological evidence, the 'new archaeologist' would argue, if rightly processed and interpreted, may indeed provide insights into the social and ideological worlds of the people who left it. Art styles and iconography, settlement patterns and building variations, should be studied to see what they may reveal of social organisation, patterns of behaviour and religious concepts in the relevant society. Encouraging as this optimism has been in stimulating fresh thought on many issues, it has yet to be cogently demonstrated that this extension of archaeological inference is really possible without some use of historical parallels or ethnographical analogies, however tentatively or obliquely they are invoked.

The more theoretical assertions and goals of the 'New Archaeology' are primarily directed to prehistory, and even then in many cases are only really applicable in the New World contexts whence they sprang. They therefore have a restricted relevance to a simple survey of the archaeologist's task in an historical situation, as in Palestine during the Bronze and Iron Ages. They also depend to some extent on a level of archaeological field research which has not yet been generally attained in Palestine.[6]

Notes

1. R. Ascher, 'Archaeology and the Public Image' in *American Antiquity* 25 (1959–60), p. 400.
2. As quoted in G. Daniel, *The Origins and Growth of Archaeology*, Harmondsworth, 1967, p. 46.
3. See W. G. Dever in J. H. Hayes and J. Maxwell Miller, *Israelite and Judaean History*, London, 1977, pp. 102ff.
4. *The Danube in Prehistory*, London, 1929, pp. v-vi.
5. *Ancient Europe*, Edinburgh, 1965, pp. 7–8.

6. For a good example of this approach see L. Marfoe, 'The Integrative Transformation: Patterns of Sociopolitical Organization in Southern Syria,' *B.A.S.O.R.* 234 (1979), pp. 1ff.

Recommended Reading

Gordon Childe, *Piecing Together the Past*, London, 1956. An important statement of method by the leading archaeological theorist of his generation.

David Clarke, *Analytical Archaeology*, 2nd revised edition; London, 1978. The impact of this pioneering book would have been greater had it been half as long and more clearly written, but selective reading in it reveals much about the aims and aspirations of the 'New Archaeology', particularly in the revised edition.

Glyn Daniel, *A Hundred and Fifty Years of Archaeology*, London, 1975. The standard history of the subject in English.

M. I. Finley, 'Archaeology and History', in *The Use and Abuse of History*, London, 1975. Although illustrated from classical sources, this important essay is very relevant to Palestinian 'historic' archaeology.

K. V. Flannery, (Ed.), *The Early Mesoamerican Village*, New York, 1976. Despite its particular geographical bias, the witty general introductions to each paper in this volume are a good plain man's guide to some of the best in recent thinking on field archaeology.

Stuart Piggott, *Approach to Archaeology*, London, 1959. A clear, elegantly written introduction to the subject from the traditional standpoint.

Roland de Vaux, 'On Right and Wrong Uses of Archaeology' in J. A. Sanders, (Ed.), *Near Eastern Archaeology in the Twentieth Century*, New York, 1970, pp. 64–80. A wise, stimulating essay on the relationship of archaeology and biblical studies.

2

The Evolution of Archaeological Method in Palestine

Exploration and ancient topography

For about fifteen hundred years from the reported quest of the Empress Helena in the early fourth century for the fragments of the true cross to the creation of the Palestine Exploration Fund in London in 1865, the ancient sites and ruins of Palestine had been haphazardly observed by a long succession of credulous pilgrims, merchants, travellers and wandering gentlemen-scholars. Not until the middle of the eighteenth century was there any attempt at accurate description and illustration of ancient monuments. With the appearance of Wood's twin volumes on the temples at Palmyra (1753) and Baalbek (1757) new standards were set, though the ruins were still romanticised in their bolder illustrations. Then for over a century or more it was travellers, rather than scholars, who unveiled one after another of the long forgotten standing monuments of antiquity in Palestine and Syria.

A fresh and profoundly significant trend was established by the Americans Edward Robinson and his travelling companion Eli Smith, a skilled Arabist, when they showed how tenaciously the old place-names of Palestine had survived in the memory of the peasant population. Although travelling only for five months in all, first in 1838 and again in 1852, they laid the essential foundations for the future study of the historical topography of Palestine through first-hand observation and sceptical appraisal of accumulated tradition. In setting to work Robinson had adopted two crucial principles. 'The *first* was to avoid as far as possible all contact with the convents and the authority of monks; to examine everywhere for ourselves with the Scriptures in our hands; and to apply for information solely to the Arab population. The *second* was to leave as much as possible the beaten track, and direct our journeys and researches to those portions of the country which had been least visited.'[1]

Throughout his travels in Palestine, though he makes regular reference to mounds and *tells* (the Arabic term for them) (see p. 43 here), Robinson never seems to have realised that they comprised the debris of successive ancient towns. Of Tell el-Hesi he wrote, 'The form of the Tell is singular, a truncated cone with a fine plain on the top. . . . From the information of our guides, and from the remarkable appearance of this isolated Tell, we had expected to find here traces of ruins. . . . Yet we could discover nothing whatever to mark the existence of any former town or structure.'[2] Ironically, in a footnote, he remarks that Felix Fabri in 1483 had reported 'thick ancient walls drawn around it,' whilst Volney had described it as artificial in his *Voyage* of 1787. Robinson, like many after him, regarded the mounds as bases or platforms for buildings, and when he found no visible ruins dismissed them.

The first men to excavate in the region were to remain equally ignorant of the true importance of *tells*. The great French biblical scholar Ernest Renan (1823–92) has the priority, though his single, incredibly productive year of research in Phoenicia from October 1860 to October 1861, involved the study of surface ruins and graves, whose excavation was little more than the clearance of debris, not deep or systematic digging. His comments on Byblos remind us forcefully how much was being damaged and destroyed in the nineteenth century. 'To build a miserable hovel the natives have destroyed curious edifices; in the search for treasure, they have demolished sanctuaries preserved intact until our day; to find a few pieces of gold, offerings of the last of the pagans, they have broken down altars and over-turned Baal from the pedestal where, I am assured, he still sat enthroned only three or four years ago!'[3] A decade later a clergyman writing from the Lebanon made the same observation in a rather different way, but of equal significance to archaeologists. 'The stones of Sidon, Tyre and Sarepta have been carried recently to Acre, Beirut and Joppa by boat in immense quantities and, after being cut afresh, and much reduced in size, are placed in buildings which, in turn, will fall to ruin in a hundred years, when the same process will be repeated until they are found no more.'[4]

Excavation came to the heart of Palestine in 1867 when the newly founded Palestine Exploration Fund despatched a young lieutenant of the Royal Engineers, Charles Warren (1840–1927), to elucidate certain vital problems in the historical topography of Jerusalem. Biblical questions at this stage dominated the programme of research with which he was entrusted; a programme so ambitious and demanding that a hundred years later the same problems concern any archaeologist working in Jerusalem. They were principally – the precise site of the temple within the Haram enclosure; the lines of the northern walls of Jerusalem; the authenticity of the Holy Sepulchre; the location of the Antonia and other places. Warren set to work in the only way he knew. 'The system adopted in excavating at Jerusalem was that ordinarily used in military mining. . . .'[5] His remarkable series of shafts and

Plate 3 Tell es-Sultan (Old Testament Jericho), looking east to the mountains of Moab.

tunnels could hardly be expected to show more than the imposing depth of ancient deposits in Jerusalem. The walls of the Haram enclosure he found descending to between 80 and 120 feet from the modern surface. Without reliable criteria for dating masonry or small finds, Warren's allotted task was wellnigh impossible, save in the most general revelation of topographical variations. What he lacked in knowledge and expertise, Warren amply compensated for in courage and enthusiasm, not completely concealed by the deadpan prose of his reports. Posterity would come to deplore his mining techniques, though he was more honest in his description than many a subsequent archaeological miner; but rarely would it match his capacity for hard work and enterprise. He subsequently made soundings in some mounds elsewhere, Tell es-Sultan (Jericho) among them, but was inclined to regard them as purely natural formations (Plate 3).

Of more far reaching and fundamental significance than the Palestine Exploration Fund's sponsorship of excavations in Jerusalem was their initiative in cartography. In 1868 with money provided by Baroness Angela

Burdett-Coutts, who wished to provide Jerusalem with a good water supply, a party of Royal Engineers, under Wilson, commenced the first modern scientific map of Palestine. A triangulation was carried along the central hills with fifty stations fixed trigonometrically and astronomically. A sketch map scaled one inch to the mile was drawn on this basis. This small-scale survey for a specific purpose clearly showed that the first step towards the scientific exploration of ancient Palestine must be the preparation of a complete survey on a large enough scale to accommodate all important features, not least the many *tells*. The Survey of Western Palestine was produced from 1871–77 covering, at one inch to the mile, from the Mediterranean to the Jordan, from Tyre and Banias in the north to Beersheba in the south. Twenty-six sheets were published in 1879. Work in Eastern Palestine from 1882 was more fragmentary, for political reasons, but no less thorough; Sinai was surveyed just before the First World War. Thus was established a tradition of accurate mapping unique in the Near East; invaluable to the proper development of field archaeology.

Excavating tells

Although from 1873 onwards German excavations at the mound of Hissarlik (Troy) in north west Turkey, directed by Schliemann, first revealed that such *tells* represented the accumulated debris of successive occupations, the discovery did not filter through to Palestine. It arrived suddenly in 1890 when the Palestine Exploration Fund commissioned a brilliant archaeologist, Flinders Petrie (1853–1942), already experienced in excavating in Egypt, to dig for them in the region east of Gaza. After eliminating two small sites, whose modern names seemed to suggest the location of biblical cities, Khirbet ʿAjlan (Eglon) and Umm Lakis (Lachish), Petrie chose to work at Tell el-Hesi nearby. 'The site', he wrote, 'was ideal for gaining a first outline of the archaeology. The stream had cut away one side of a mound of ruin sixty feet thick, and I could begin by terracing along each level and getting out its pottery. . . .

The successive walls could be distinguished, and the outline of the great early fortification round the hill. . . . Then, with the dating of the pottery that had been obtained, I went over southern Judaea, estimating the age and prospects of each of the ancient sites.'[6]

Petrie's six weeks of work at Hesi, crude as it may now seem to anyone using his characteristically rapid publication, laid secure and fundamental foundations for future excavations in its emphasis on isolating the individual layers of occupation with their distinctive types of pottery. Even at this stage Petrie was able to use his knowledge of Egyptian pottery from dated tombs to suggest dates for comparable wares at Hesi. When Egyptian scarabs (seals) and inscriptions with royal names were associated with pottery, it was possible to turn a relative chronology into an approximate absolute chronology in years BC using the Egyptian system (see p. 72ff.). Although an American, Bliss, continued excavations at Hesi when Petrie returned to Egypt, he did not correlate thorough descriptions of pottery with his observations of the various levels nor did he publish his results in the detail that Petrie's methods required. It was a classic demonstration, if demonstration were needed, that there is no substitute for a master excavator of one generation instructing his successors over a period of years in the field. In Egypt Petrie was to establish such a legacy of supervisors and native workmen. In Palestine it is little exaggeration to say that his absence held method back for a generation. When he returned in the 1920s he was too old, too fixed in his ways and too aloof to make a significant contribution to techniques of excavation.

Meanwhile a more rudimentary method of working was evident in Macalister's excavations at Gezer, in the years 1902–9, where he worked on a huge scale single-handed, save for large parties of local labourers. He is

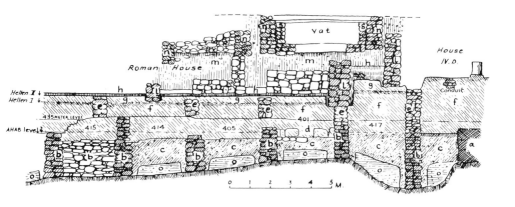

Figure 2 Reisner's drawing of the superimposed building levels in the mound at Samaria. E-W section through S4E; *a*, western face of main building of Ahab; *b*, walls of the Ostraca House; *o*, mason's debris on rock; *c*, filling of Ahab's courtyard; *d*, reconstruction of Ostraca House; *e*, Greek or Hellenistic walls; *f*, double layer of debris, the lower part of which was disturbed Israelite debris; *g*, two preherodian floors just beneath *h*, which was the floor of the Herodian Atrium House; *l*, boundary walls of a Herodian street; *m*, debris in Atrium House; *n* and *s*, walls of the period of Severus. (After G. A. Reisner, *Harvard Excavations at Samaria 1908-9*, Cambridge, Mass., 1924, figure 14.)

estimated to have excavated about 60% of the mound to bedrock and cleared 250 tombs. The recent American excavations at Gezer were concentrated on about 1.75% of the *tell*. Macalister's monumental publication is packed with objects and observations, but without due regard to their proper sequence and association with buildings. Indeed a gap in occupation in the Iron Age was missed, leading to an erroneous 'correction' of the ceramic chronology established by Bliss at Hesi. The architectural features of Gezer were only schematically treated and the levelling and surveying were far from adequate. In contrast German excavators of the period at such major sites as Megiddo, Jericho and Taanach, laid great emphasis on architectural analysis, with meticulous building plans and photographs. But, as there was no attempt to relate them to the levels of occupational and other debris whence they came, chronological relationships remained very much of a mystery.

Then in 1908 another talented field archaeologist from Egypt, this time the American George Reisner (1867–1942) came briefly to Palestine, where he brilliantly analysed the special problems of digging a mound in the hill

25

country, before returning to Egypt. Reisner's excavations at Samaria (1909–10), or more exactly his account of his methods printed in 1924, have been taken to mark a watershed in the evolution of field archaeology in the area.[7] Linked with the name of his collaborator C. S. Fisher (1876–1941), his approach has been taken to exemplify a distinct new methodology, the *Reisner-Fisher* (or *locus to architecture*) method. The extent to which Reisner actually used the techniques implied by his report, when digging nearly twenty years earlier, is much debated. Undoubtedly his published remarks on the complex structure of a *tell* go much further than anything Petrie ever printed and, in many places, describe methods for unravelling it now widely used. His emphasis on adequate trained staff, on detailed records, on accurate plans and photographs, are all now commonplace. Yet when Fisher himself later came to describe in detail in a publication of 1929[8] the methods he used at Megiddo (Plate 4) the practices advocated seem closer to those of the German architectural school than to Reisner's most original ideas. Fisher made virtually no mention of the varied layers in a *tell* and wrote very much as the trained architect he was. Excavation was seen as a matter of clearing and plotting walls and rooms, with objects recorded in relation to their absolute position within a room. Whole areas were to be excavated down to arbitrary depths, and the walls planned in relation to one another, without reference to the debris interleaving them or to the many intrusive features which complicated their chronological relationships – all matters clearly discussed by Reisner in 1924.

When Albright (1891–1971) began work at Tell Beit Mirsim in 1926 he certainly considered himself to be applying the Reisner-Fisher method, though he footnoted a revealingly sharp criticism of it. 'Of course, this method is only sound when applied with adequate knowledge of pottery and comparative archaeology; otherwise it may conceal thoroughly unsound execution and interpretation.'[9] That Albright brought to Tell Beit Mirsim 'an adequate knowledge of comparative archaeology' is evident in his work, and that he evolved there the basis for all subsequent study of the pottery of Palestine over thousands of years is equally clear; but what is not so clear is his method of work and the means he used to avoid the practical shortcomings of his predecessors. As none of his publications of Tell Beit Mirsim contains a sectional drawing to show the interrelations of earth, occupational debris and structures in the mound, his innovations must be sought elsewhere.

His emphasis on the sorting and dating of pottery was crucial. Each arbitrarily defined unit (or locus) of excavation, be it part of a room, below a floor, beside a wall, was considered in terms of the pottery found there. This was analysed into distinctive types, then loci which yielded the same

Plate 4 Megiddo: view of the American excavations of the 1930s as preserved in 1970; the so-called 'bamah' in the foreground.

types, and the structures of which they formed part were allocated to the same building period (or stratum). One basic point about this way of digging needs to be stressed here to draw out an important point of contrast with the method next used in Palestine. In Albright's system the unit of excavation, or the locus, described the limits of a convenient area of work arbitrarily defined; it is not primarily defined in terms of observable layers of debris. This is immediately clear in the sectional drawings Albright did publish. They are not drawings of observed levels in the side of a trench. They are diagrams drawn after excavation showing the relationship of one wall to another in terms of loci producing similar pottery. To the non-specialist this may seem a narrow distinction, but an important corollary follows. In Albright's method the word *stratum* usually means a series of buildings assumed by the excavator to be contemporary on the evidence of the pottery found in them. It is an artificial division within the makeup of a mound rather than an observed one. The primary geological meaning of the word *stratum*, an observed division in layers of rock or debris, is that fundamental to the most influential of all methods of excavation now used in Palestine, that long associated with the names of Mortimer Wheeler (1890–1976) and Kathleen Kenyon (1906–1978).

After training on Romano-British excavations in England with Wheeler, Miss Kenyon applied his techniques to Samaria where she was a member of the Joint Expedition (1931–5) under J. W. Crowfoot. Samaria, as Reisner had found, is a singularly complex site, since deep and very substantial Hellenistic and Roman foundations have destroyed so much of the earlier building by kings of Israel from Omri to the Assyrian sack of 722/1 BC. Miss Kenyon cut a trench through the northern side of the mound summit to unravel the chronology of the successive building periods and their associated pottery. Her account of her methods, in a lecture published in 1939, provides an appropriate, succinct description of the fundamentals in the *Wheeler-Kenyon* (or *baulk/debris-layer*) approach.

It is quite clear that to go straight ahead and clear out all the soil would destroy all the evidence. It would be useless to record the absolute depth of the objects, since in different parts of the site this has a different significance, and it may well have arrived in its position by a foundation trench or a robber trench cutting through the earlier levels. It is necessary, therefore to examine and correlate all the layers of soil, particularly in relation to the walls. Therefore, the worst possible thing to do is to clear along the face of a wall, as its relation to the layers is thus destroyed. It is necessary to cut a section at right angles to each wall, in order to decide which layers are earlier, contemporary and so on. The next stage is to secure sections across the whole area, linking it all together. The method of digging therefore is to start by cutting trenches across the area in order to identify floors and foundation trenches and robber trenches. When the meaning of a layer has been established and complete records have been made, by planning, photographing and drawing sections, it can then be removed, care of course being taken to keep separate material from the foundation trenches and robber trenches. . . . For the purposes of identification later, it is of course necessary that full notes should be kept as to where everything comes from. . . .[10]

Only one crucial aspect of the Wheeler-Kenyon method is not made clear by this extract. We must introduce it at once as much subsequent negative

Plate 5 *Opposite*: Aerial view of Tell es-Sultan, showing Kathleen Kenyon's deep cutting (trench A) and wider area excavations.

reaction to this method in Palestine turns on it. Miss Kenyon herself described it with characteristic firmness in 1952. 'It is therefore an absolute principle of excavation, which allows of no exceptions at all, that the whole area must not be cleared simultaneously. Standing sections must be left at frequent intervals from the surface down, and it must be possible to relate all structures or disturbances to them.'[11] It is these 'standing sections' (or baulks), which must be drawn in the field with great care, that have inhibited many archaeologists otherwise sympathetic to the main premise of this technique. Her method requires that the successive layers of a mound are peeled off in accord with their proper bed-lines, thus ensuring the accurate isolation of structural phases and related artefacts, and recorded on the spot by drawing.

It was not until the Kenyon excavations at Jericho (Plate 5) from 1952–58 that these methods became properly known in Palestine and it was not until the 1960s that they were being widely used in some form or other by fellow archaeologists. Their reception was far from uncritical and often slow, as national rivalries and political circumstances tended to isolate excavators at the time. Personal contacts through participation in excavations in progress are vital to the rapid and accurate dissemination of new techniques, since full archaeological publications are always long delayed and rarely describe field methods explicitly.

The first large-scale American application of the Wheeler-Kenyon method was at Shechem from 1956–9 by G. E. Wright (1909–74). This was as crucial a training school for a new generation of field archaeologists as the Kenyon excavations in Jericho and later in Jerusalem. Subsequent American expeditions have used her method, often with distinctive modifications, at such major sites as Ai, Gezer, Hesi, Jemmeh and Taanach. The major American departures from Kenyon's own field practice have been in a more extended use of teams in the actual direction of the excavation, in an ever wider involvement of natural scientists with sieving and flotation techniques used for the proper recovery of bone and seed samples, and in more elaborate systems for recovering and recording pottery. The Gezer expedition of the early 1970s for instance had a staff of about thirty professionals including, in addition to archaeologists, palaeo-botanists, palaeo-zoologists, physical anthropologists, cultural anthropologists, art historians, geologists, ecologists, computer programmers and historians of technology. In the application of the baulk/debris-layer technique a conscious effort has been made to apply it to wide horizontal areas in contrast to the deep vertical cuts in long trenches used at Jericho and Jerusalem. Although the Wheeler-Kenyon method is pre-eminently suited to unravelling a *tell*'s history by trenching through many superimposed levels, American work has undoubtedly shown

Plate 6 Beersheba: aerial view of the excavation of the Iron Age town; the modern camp gives some idea of the scale of the ancient town.

that with sufficient responsible, trained supervisors and financial resources, it is equally appropriate for wide exposures, especially on briefly occupied settlement sites.

Among Israeli archaeologists, where the best of the architectural tradition exemplified by 'Munya' Dunayevsky (1906–68) has persisted more strongly, the Wheeler-Kenyon method has been less readily accepted. The publications of Yadin's excavation at Hazor, for example, illustrate very well the large-scale application of a primarily architectural approach. In general Israeli archaeologists have preferred horizontal exposures of considerable size for which they regard the Wheeler-Kenyon method, with its all important baulks, as too restricting. Aharoni argued particularly that this method neglected architecture and vessels of pottery found *in situ*. At Arad and Beersheba, believing that only vessels from floor levels were stratigraphically reliable, he laid great emphasis on the restoration of complete pots and recorded his pottery finds accordingly (Plates 6,9). He used baulks sparingly and very flexibly, regarding the drawing of them in the field as an unnecessary, indeed subjective, exercise. He preferred to draw them subsequently from photographs taken on site. No one who has ever drawn a section on site would deny that it is an exercise as much in interpretation as in observation, and should therefore if possible be done through two or more sets of eyes; but it is this very fact that makes it so crucial to the debris–layer method. It is this meticulous, on the spot, checking and rechecking of the section *in situ* (and drawing is the keenest form of observation) that ensures as far as humanly possible the correct peeling of one layer of debris from another, with the concomitant proper chronological association of structural phases and artefacts. Recent developments suggest a growing assimilation of the Wheeler-Kenyon and the Israeli approaches, notably at Tell ed-Duweir (Lachish).[12]

Site survey

Once the real significance of the numerous Palestinian *tells* had been recognised, there was no obstacle to their ready location and recognition, though identifying their ancient names might prove highly complex. But not all archaeological sites in Palestine are mounds, conspicuous to the eye. Although as early as 1890 (see p. 24) Petrie had recognised the significance of pottery sherds in surface survey, it was not until Nelson Glueck (1900–71) launched his remarkable systematic archaeological surveys of Transjordan in 1932 that the technique received its fullest application. These surveys ran until political circumstances stopped them in 1947. Glueck then undertook, from 1952 until the time of his death, an equally extensive survey in the Negev. There are scarcely any true mounds in these areas, since density and continuity of village settlement needs more rainfall than is available. Through detailed study of pottery sherds collected from the surface of ancient sites Glueck was able, in forty years of strenuous travelling, to outline a provisional, comprehensive picture of the process of settlement, particularly its ebb and flow, in Gilead, Ammon, Moab, Edom, the Negev and deserts of Sinai. Such methods of survey and mapping are now a commonplace of archaeological fieldwork, but it is unlikely that such intensity of research will ever again be achieved by one man. Teams working small areas intensively are now preferred. Nor did Glueck neglect the importance of cross-checking his survey results through excavation, though the two sites he dug had been originally discovered by others. In the late 1930s he excavated a Nabataean temple at Khirbet et-Tannur and an Iron Age fort at Tell el-Kheleifeh (?Ezion-Geber).

A number of scientific techniques devised for other purposes have contributed significantly to the development of archaeological survey. Towards the end of the First World War a unit under German leadership was formed in the Turkish army fighting on the Palestinian Front for the protection of monuments. Its commander, Theodor Wiegand, later to be president of the German Archaeological Institute, realised how useful aerial photographs would be for his mission. Photographs taken then of the Negev by Oberleutnant Falke were published in 1920; among the first such photographs deliberately taken for an archaeological purpose. They immediately revealed the enormous potential of this technique in studying the desert and semi-desert periphery of Palestine and Syria. Ruined villages, forts, monasteries, towns, field and water systems, roads and tracks immediately showed up. Such photographs were later used by Glueck and are now a constant frame of reference for surface surveys, not only on land; as indeed are satellite photographs.

One of the pioneers of aerial research in Syria, Père Poidebard, also used it most ingeniously in the 1930s in association with surface and underwater surveys to study ancient port installations at Tyre.[13] In recent years underwater archaeology has been systematically developed. It now regularly contributes to knowledge both of harbour installations along the east Mediterranean coast and of ancient ships, through the identification and subsequent excavation of wrecks. The earliest of these wrecks so far fully published, investigated in 1960, was the remains of a merchant ship sailing westwards from a port in Cyprus or Syria about 1200 BC.[14] It had been driven on to Cape Gelidonya in southern Turkey, with a cargo of ingots and scrap metal. Other wrecks, or ancient cargoes dumped in storms, are at present under investigation off the coast of Israel.

The predominance of the *tell* in Palestine, for which the techniques are not best suited, have restricted the use of magnetic surveying in this area; but its potential on level sites of relatively short occupation is as important here as elsewhere and has already been demonstrated on a few sites.[15] Since the 1950s instruments and principles evolved for geological prospecting have been adapted for archaeological use. The proton magnetometer and its related instruments are used to detect such buried remains as iron objects, fired structures, like kilns, ovens and hearths, pits and ditches filled with rubbish, and, in certain circumstances, walls, foundations, tombs and roads. The detection of iron by magnetic prospecting needs no explanation here. The other cases are more subtle. The disturbances they offer are much weaker and arise because of slight magnetic effects produced by fire and high humus content. With the proton magnetometer an acre may be covered in about four hours, depending naturally on the number of features located. This method is faster and easier than the detection of buried archaeological remains by measurement of the electrical resistivity of the soil, used in geological surveying since the second decade of this century, but not applied archaeologically until the later 1940s. Since resistivity surveys are most conveniently made in straight lines, they are most suited to linear features such as ditches, and are more reliable for the detection of stone structures generally. As research in Palestine moves increasingly to smaller sites of brief occupation such survey methods as these will become routine aids to excavation as elsewhere in the world.

Notes

1. *Biblical Researches in Palestine, Mount Sinai and Arabia Petraea* I, London, 1841, p. 377.
2. Op. cit., II, p. 390.
3. As cited in F. J. Bliss, *The Development of Palestine Exploration*, London, 1906, p. 251.
4. W. M. Thompson, *The Land and the Book*, London, 1870, p. 110.
5. In W. Morrison (Ed.), *The Recovery of Jerusalem*, London, 1871, p. 56.
6. *Seventy Years in Archaeology*, London, 1937, p. 117.
7. *Harvard Excavations at Samaria* I, Cambridge, Mass.
8. *The Excavation of Armageddon*, Oriental Institute Communications 4, Chicago 1929, pp. 26 ff.
9. *The Excavation of Tell Beit Mirsim* II: *The Bronze Age*, A.A.S.O.R. (1938), p. 8, footnote; also on his own methods, *Bibliotheca Orientalis*, XXI (1964), p. 69.

10. P.E.Q. (1939), pp. 34–5.
11. *Beginning in Archaeology*, London, 1952, p. 77.
12. D. Ussishkin, 'Excavations at Tel Lachish 1973–77, *Tel Aviv* 5 (1978), pp. 1ff.
13. *Un grand port disparu: Tyre*, Paris, 1939.
14. G. F. Bass, *Cape Gelidonya: A Bronze Age Shipwreck*, Philadelphia, 1967.
15. A. Hesse, 'Applications de Méthodes Géophysiques de Prospection à l'étude de sites préhistoriques et protohistoriques', in *Paléorient* I (1973), pp. 11–20.

Recommended Reading

There is no modern history of archaeological research in Palestine. The early years are covered by F. J. Bliss, *The Development of Palestinian Exploration*, London, 1906; R. A. S. Macalister, *A Century of Excavation in Palestine*, London, 1925.

The following is a selection of the more important books and papers dealing with method in Palestine, sometimes in historical perspective.

Y. Aharoni, 'Methods of recording and documentation' in *Beersheba* I, Tel Aviv, 1973, pp. 119–132.
W. G. Dever, 'Two Approaches to Archaeological Method – the Architectural and the Stratigraphic', 1 in *Eretz-Israel* 11 (1973), pp. 1*–8*.
Nelson Glueck, *Rivers in the Desert*, London, 1959; *The Other Side of the Jordan*, Cambridge, Mass., 1970.
K. M. Kenyon 'Excavating Methods in Palestine,' in *P.E.Q.*, (1939), pp. 29–37. *Beginning in Archaeology*, London, 2nd Edn., 1953. This is a general survey with no particular reference to Palestine.
L. E. Toombs, 'Principles of Field Technique' in G. E. Wright, *Shechem*, London, 1965, pp. 185–190.
R. E. M. Wheeler, *Archaeology from the Earth*, Oxford, 1954.
G. E. Wright, 'Archaeological Method in Palestine – An American Interpretation', in *Eretz-Israel* IX (1969), pp. 125–9.
G. R. H. Wright, 'A Method of Excavation Common in Palestine' in *Zeitschrift des Deutschen Palästina-Vereins* 82 (1966), 113–135.

3

Towards Excavation

The exploration of Western Palestine at least, is almost exhausted on the surface, but there is a great future for it under-ground. We have run most of the questions to earth; it only remains to dig them up.

George Adam Smith, 1894.

Site Identification

The quest for 'biblical sites' was long the mainspring of archaeological research in Palestine. Although archaeological search and survey now have different goals, even in those historical periods covered by Old Testament narratives, Palestine is so rich in information on its ancient place-names that archaeology will never be wholly free of text-aided topography west of the Jordan. For this reason a sharp distinction must immediately be drawn between an 'archaeological' map and the 'historical' or 'biblical' maps of Palestine most familiar to students of the region. A map designed to illustrate the occupation of Palestine in the Late Bronze Age, c. 1550–1200 BC, will mark those spots where material remains of this period have been identified, using modern placenames or co-ordinates to identify them. By contrast comparison of various versions of a map of the region 'in the time of Joshua and Judges' will reveal marked discrepancies in the location of certain biblical place-names. This is because biblical sites, unlike archaeological ones, may only be located on the ground through often complex arguments involving philology, history, archaeology and topography, and the evidence is by no means always decisive. The Israelite sanctuary of Gilgal, to take an extreme example, at different times has been located within a short distance of Jericho at such disparate archaeological sites as various Iron Age farms, a Roman villa, a Byzantine church and an Early Islamic palace.

It may surprise many people to hear that only about half the place-names given in the Bible, about 260 sites in all, are at present identified on the ground with any confidence. Significantly, nearly 200 of these preserve their ancient name, or else it survives somewhere in the vicinity of the mound which is all that now survives of the ancient settlement. A mere 70 sites have been identified without any such guidance and many of these identifications are necessarily conjectural. They will remain so until inscriptions found on them, or at adjacent sites, sharply reduce the range of possibilities in the arguments for identity. These have to accommodate themselves to information drawn from the study of Arabic place-names, from geographical identifications in historical texts of various periods, from the Bible itself, from topographical conditions in the most likely area, and ultimately from data revealed by excavation. All must be consonant to inspire any confidence in the proposed identification.

Unlike Jerusalem or Tyre, few biblical towns have been continuously occupied since antiquity. Most of them are now no more than mounds of earth and rubble, often some distance from modern areas of settlement. A few retain names immediately reminiscent of their ancient one (Dibon = Dhiban); but the majority do not. Modern names may sometimes sound like ancient ones and yet have no connection with the like sounding biblical one (Umm Lakis, near Tell el-Hesi, see below), whilst ancient biblical names were transferred in time from one settlement to another. Thus the name Jericho is preserved in that of the modern village er-Riha, near which lies the mound of Tell es-Sultan, with a spring, accepted as the site of the Old Testament town. New Testament Jericho lies some distance away at modern Khirbet en-Nitla.

Precise confirmation by archaeology of biblical site locations is rare. Two unusually direct examples will show how unpredictable it can be. As early as the seventeenth century the village of el-Jib, 9 kilometres north of Jerusalem, was identified textually as the site of ancient Gibeon. This was strikingly confirmed during excavations there in the later 1950s when pottery wine-jars were found stamped with the ancient name 'Gibeon' (see p. 90). Their number, and associated evidence to indicate that the jars were being filled on the spot, virtually ruled out the possibility that they were imports from elsewhere. In the nineteenth century the great biblical scholar Clermont-Ganneau reading an Arab chronicler's account of how the noise of a skirmish about AD 1525 in the region of Ramleh had been heard in the village of Khuldeh and at Tell el-Jazar, was struck by the similarity of this name to Hebrew Gezer. Tell el-Jazar is about 8 kilometres south-south-east of Ramleh. Rock-cut boundary inscriptions were subsequently discovered in the vicinity of the mound, including the phrase 'boundary of Gezer' in Hebrew and giving in the Greek genitive the name Alkios, of its owner or administrator in the Herodian period.

The role of archaeology in a more complex instance illustrates the great

Plate 7   Tell el-Husn (ancient Bethshan) seen behind the Roman theatre.

care needed in correlating the diverse evidence for identification. In the course of his researches Robinson (p. 20), having found mention of Tell el-Hesi in Crusader literature, speculated whether a ruin called Umm Lakis, 5 kilometres north-west of the Tell, might have been biblical Lachish. He decided not on account of its small size and location, which did not seem to correspond with the requirements of the ancient written sources. About 2½ kilometres north of Tell el-Hesi is another ruin, known as Khirbet ʿAjlan, which Robinson took to be identical with biblical Eglon. Almost sixty years later, in 1890, Petrie briefly examined these two ruins, finding them to be Roman or later, before moving to Tell el-Hesi (p. 24). He appreciated, as Robinson had not, that this was the remains of an ancient city. But was it Lachish or was it Eglon? Petrie assumed the former, as seemed to be

38

confirmed two years later when Bliss found there a tablet naming Zimrida, governor of Lachish in the fourteenth century BC.

In 1924 Albright challenged this assumption, arguing that, in view of its size and situation, Tell el-Hesi was biblical Eglon. In 1929 he identified Tell ed-Duweir, further inland, as the site of ancient Lachish, 'this general location suits the biblical references to the place remarkably well, while Tell el-Hesi does not. Tell ed-Duweir is easily four times as large as the latter, which is altogether too small to represent an important Jewish town like Lachish.'² In 1935 during British excavations at Tell ed-Duweir tablets found in the early sixth century destruction debris of a gateway in the city wall seemed to confirm Albright's surmise. Letter IV in this group, written to the commander at headquarters from an officer in an outpost reads in part, 'We are watching for the signals of Lachish . . . for we cannot see Azekah.'[3] This archive has been associated with the recorded sack of Lachish by the Babylonian army of Nebuchadnezzar II in 587/6 BC. The junior officer is assumed to be reporting to his superior in the city of Lachish (Tell ed-Duweir), where the tablet was then filed in an office within the gate. Renewed excavations at Tell el-Hesi have not yet confirmed that it was Eglon.

Site survey

Contemporary archaeologists in Palestine are no longer pre-occupied with major biblical signposts to the country's ancient settlement patterns. Comprehensive, systematic surveys in carefully selected regions have largely replaced random, haphazard surveys round excavations on major biblical sites. Any well considered programme of archaeological field survey is now based on a careful appraisal of every aspect of the natural environment in the area to be studied, the economic factors likely to have affected its exploitation at various periods, and as full a knowledge as is possible of the region's history. When the archaeological landscape is not so well defined as in the heartland of Palestine, the archaeologist must start from scratch in the manner pioneered by Glueck in Transjordan and the Negev (see pp. 32f.).

Less well known is the case of P.L.O. Guy whose archaeological researches in the Negev in 1937–8 stimulated subsequent interest in the application of ancient methods of water conservation and soil preservation to the re-establishment of agrricultural communities there.[4] These are areas with relatively few *tells*, little or no documentary evidence, and complex problems of water supply directly affecting the patterns of human settlement. In such circumstances the archaeological investigator depends on a sharp eye, sturdy legs and a sound, but flexible appreciation of topography, gleaned from preliminary work on maps and air photographs, and a good knowledge of pottery chronology. The more ambitious the project, the wider will be the range of natural scientists drawn in to make specialist reports complementary to the archaeological search for material vestiges of ancient occupation.

Although landscapes vary markedly in Palestine, as has man's response to them, the archaeologist on survey directs his attention first to the fundamental factors which have always controlled settlement – water and lines of communication. It is no accident that many of the most famous ancient cities of Palestine, Gezer, Gibeon, Hazor, Jerusalem, Lachish and Megiddo, are distinguished by the elaborate fortifications of their water supplies. Strings of settlements commonly follow the line of stream beds, particularly when

Plate 8   Tell ed-Duweir: east wall of Late Bronze Age temple.

they have a continuous rather than a seasonal flow of water. In the Negev, for instance, wells were dug along river beds (*wadis*), where they could be filled by winter floods; only at Beersheba was a well sunk on the *tell* itself. Nor are sources of water always obvious. Sub-surface water to be found by digging shallow holes was not neglected in antiquity (2 Kings 3:16–17) and the archaeologist must be alive to all possibilities.

Many ancient means of water supply and conservation in the region have been rediscovered by archaeologists and hydrologists working in close collaboration. The ancient and modern water supplies at one place are not necessarily identical. The outlets of springs may sometimes change due to alterations in the sub-surface limestone formation. At Megiddo there is now no spring near the mouth of the ancient water tunnel that leads into the city, though there are two elsewhere at the foot of the mound. When considering water supplies the archaeologist does well to bear certain natural limitations in mind. Without the support of a relatively developed technology for water storage and conservation many of the peripheral areas of Syro-Palestine, which might otherwise seem so, are not suitable for agricultural exploitation where the rainfall is below a regular 200–300 mm each year. But, like the large flat plains of the Beersheba region where the high water table is accessible to shallow wells, they may be particularly well suited to pastoral communities. In contrast there are regions where there is less than 100 mm of annual rainfall, as in parts of the Negev, capable of supporting agricultural communities through relatively simple catchment systems and terraces in rocky valleys.

Natural lines of communication, like water sources, are key indicators to potential areas of ancient settlement. A continuous line of ancient towns and villages marks out the 'Via Maris' along the Palestinian coast from Sinai northwards into Syria. No less clear, if less numerous, are those along the line of the 'King's Highway' to the east of the Dead Sea and the river Jordan, where readily fortified positions attracted settlers most particularly when there was a water supply. But many smaller signs have also to be carefully sought and assessed by the archaeologist when on survey. Human adaptation to landscape may in antiquity have taken forms no longer current in the area of investigation and thus be unpredictable. Distinctive vegetation on recently abandoned settlements may be a clue to locating much older sites that this vegetation also favours. Also, vegetation commonly flourishes more vigorously where the subsoil has been disturbed. Ploughed fields more readily reveal traces of buildings, ash or artefacts than untilled land. Natural exposures through erosion or man-made cuts for roads or canals can reveal sites unrecognisable from the surface. Earth thrown up by burrowing animals may also offer indicative artefacts from well below the surface. Conversations with local inhabitants about tales of buried treasure or bones, about local names for unusual features, and about folklore in general may throw up unexpected clues to ancient sites.

As far as *tells* are concerned a trained eye can estimate with some degree of accuracy the type of settlement which they conceal. Woolley, whose skill in selecting sites for excavation was outstanding, has left a succinct description of this. 'Even without excavating one can distinguish something of the nature of the North Syrian *tells*. There is the simple tumulus-like mound which represents probably a small village or an isolated fort; there is a longer mound, flat-topped and rather fan-shaped, rising to a higher knoll at its narrow end, which is the village commanded by the head-man's house or fortress; there is the cup-shaped mound, hollow in the centre and with a depression in one side of its rim, which is the walled town with its gateway; and, on a bigger scale . . . the wide ring of the earth rampart enclosing the town ruins and the high acropolis hill.'[5]

The archaeologist engaged on survey is seeking two major kinds of information. First, he is trying to establish within broad limits the character and distribution of ancient settlements by mapping and distinguishing major from minor settlements, towns from farms, forts from homesteads, isolated shrines from burial grounds. Second, usually through pottery sherds on the surface, he attempts to establish their date of occupation. By drawing up distribution maps of sites with a predominance of particular types of pottery, or occasionally other objects, he will hope to define, very approximately, periods of occupation. But he must be cautious. The handling of pottery from survey is always a difficult matter before studies in depth, through excavation, have been conducted in the same area to check chronological details. Surface pottery may be misleading as an indicator of the range of periods represented on a particular site, emphasising some, obscuring others. The most that may be expected is a good correspondence between surface indications and the upper levels of a site when excavated. The archaeologist surveying new territory is always at the mercy of his own knowledge and experience. Glueck working in Transjordan, for example, has been criticised for only publishing those sherds, and then not in sufficient detail, which he recognised from familiarity with sites west of the river Jordan. This sometimes concealed the distinctive character of Transjordanian pottery in certain periods (see below).

Surveys are increasingly as much an instrument of research in their own right as they are a necessary adjunct to excavation. They provide the primary hypotheses about the development of human society in any area to be tested by selective excavation. The contrasting distribution of various pottery types will reflect cultural relationships between different areas. Detailed study of

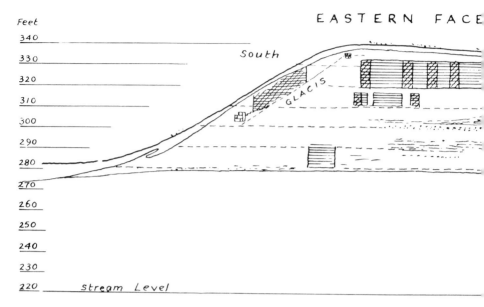

Figure 3 Petrie's drawing of the stratigraphy in Tell el-Hesi (1890). (After W. M. F. Petrie, *Tell el Hesy (Lachish)*, London, 1891, plate III, upper.)

settlement size and distribution will allow comparative densities of population at different periods to be broadly gauged. Contrasts between settlement types, agricultural, urban or military, will suggest conclusions about the purpose and progress of settlement in virgin territory. The alignment and disposition of settlements will indicate primary lines of communication and potential trading contacts. Above all, and in greatest contrast with the traditional approach, conspicuous *tells*, those until recently the ones invariably excavated, are seen as part of a system, as one link in a complex network of political, social and economic relationships through which the area was exploited by man at various times in antiquity.

No survey is ever definitive. The same ground covered by one expert may be resurveyed by another later, and new information gathered. Fresh eyes concerned with different problems will detect things unnoticed before. Wind and rain are constantly exposing new surfaces and with them fresh traces of ancient occupation. Regular resurveying is above all a crucial check on negative conclusions. With what authority may it be said after survey, that a certain area was *not* inhabited at a particular period? How are the presence and movement of nomadic and semi-nomadic peoples in antiquity to be detected and plotted? Important historical conclusions have been drawn

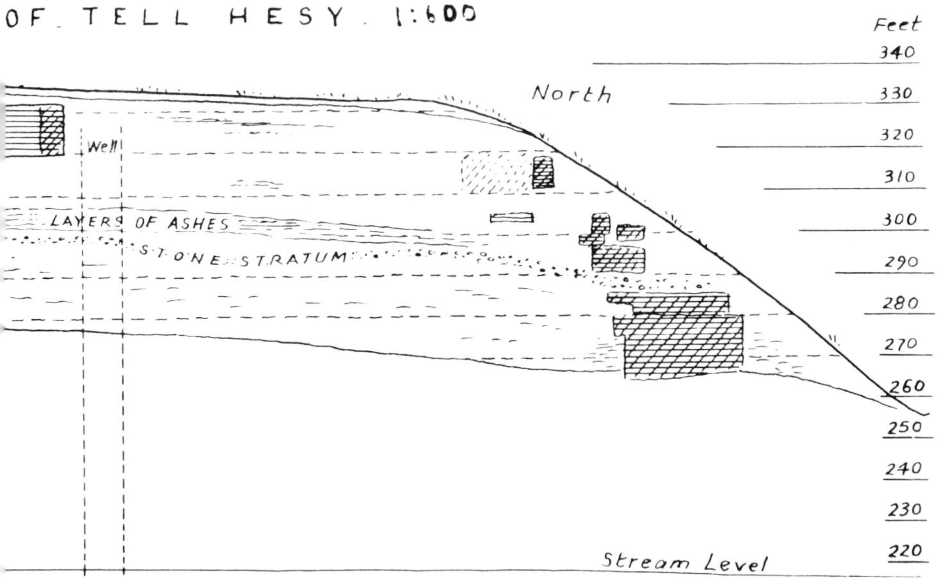

Feet
340
330
North
320
310
300
290
280
270
260
250
240
230
220

Well

LAYERS OF ASHES

STONE STRATUM

Stream Level

from arguments *ex silentio* and the archaeologist, as his knowledge increases through controlled excavation, must all the time check back on the settlement patterns established by earlier field surveys to be sure that negative evidence still stands.

This is particularly well illustrated by recent re-assessments of Glueck and Albright's hypothesis that after relatively dense agricultural settlement during the Middle Bronze I much of Transjordan was devoid of settled population and passed under nomadic control for most of the second millennium BC. This interpretation rested on the absence of Middle and Late Bronze Age pottery from Glueck's survey collections. Subsequent research and survey have shown that the gap in Glueck's material was not so much a reflection of the real situation as an indication both of the limited nature of his pioneering forays into Transjordan, in which one man covered vast areas, and of his lack of familiarity with the local pottery of the Middle and Late Bronze Ages. Small village farming communities, it now seems, were typical of the Transjordanian Bronze Age throughout. This new understanding has important implications for the use of archaeological data in any attempt to give the Patriarchal narratives a historical context.[6]

In the last decade a fresh form of survey has increasingly established itself

Plate 9 Tell Arad: part of the Early Bronze Age town in course of excavation.

in Palestinian archaeology. The landscape round the great *tells* of Palestine, excavated in the years between Petrie's work at Tell el-Hesi in 1890 and the enormous expansion of archaeological research after 1950, plays very little part in the published reports. Petrie was almost alone when in his account of excavations at Tell Jemmeh, in his volume titled *Gerar* (1928), he provided a commentary on the mound's relation to local geology and integrated it with historical and archaeological evidence. This absence of interest in the natural environment may well strike the layman as curious, when so many Palestinian sites now lie in regions no longer settled or cultivated (Jeremiah 51:43); their barrenness often contrasting vividly with the extent and splendour of the ruins. In such circumstances the curious naturally inquire

whether the landscape has always been like that, and if so, why men settled there, and if not what was it once like and why has it changed. Once it was accepted that natural scientists were a necessary and integral part of field research in archaeology such questions began to receive the consideration they deserve. The ancient settlement pattern is now studied as part of the ancient landscape, whose reconstruction is attempted through the geological history of the contemporary environment correlated with the evidence for ancient conditions provided by such things as seeds, pollen, bones, shells, etc. recovered from various levels in local excavations (see pp. 105ff. here).

The survey of contemporary land forms, of sediments, of land usage and of the exploitation of mineral resources is slowly evolving its own methodology suited to the investigation of the ancient environment. One such approach, pioneered for prehistoric sites in Palestine, has paid particular attention to the relationships between ancient technologies and those natural resources lying within economic range of individual settlements. Walking time rather than walking distance provides the crucial factor in establishing this primary zone of exploitation. Such survey has become known as 'site catchment analysis', by analogy with river drainage or with the zones from which schools are intended to draw their pupils. If geomorphology has much to contribute to understanding man's exploitation of his natural setting in antiquity, the role of climate in his fortunes is less easily established. Although often invoked as an explanation for major changes in settlement patterns, attempts to set studies of ancient climatic variations on a sound footing of research have met with mixed success.[7] In the marginal areas of Palestine which concern the archaeologist most in this respect, ecologically significant minor climatic variations in antiquity may have left little or no physical traces which may now be recognised.

Selecting a site for excavation

The commonest question addressed to archaeologists the world over is, 'Why are you digging here?' Not so long ago the answer in Palestine would have been given simply by naming the site and referring to its role in the Old Testament. The choice of Tell el-Hesi by Petrie in 1890 was exceptional. Pioneer excavations at Jerusalem, Jericho, Gezer, Megiddo, Samaria and many other sites were more mainstream 'biblical' choices. At such sites the aim was to uncover as much of the ancient town as possible with particular attention to aspects relevant to its biblical history. The tradition persists. Many of the major Palestinian mounds have been re-investigated since the Second World War, but new aims have also emerged. Yadin chose Tell el-Qedah (Hazor) in 1956 not only because Galilee was relatively unknown archaeologically, but 'for other compelling reasons as well: the important role played by the city in the history of the country in biblical times; its enormous size and peculiar features, unparalleled by any other site in the country; and the abundance of references to it in extra-biblical sources covering a period from the second millennium BC . . . making Hazor almost unique among Palestinian cities.'[8] When Miss Kenyon returned to Jericho in 1952, sixteen years after Garstang ended his work there, it was 'to obtain additional information on the date of the fall of the latest Bronze Age city, presumably to be associated with the Israelite invasion under Joshua, to clear a further area of the very important Neolithic remains discovered by

Plate 10   View into the rock-cut Middle Bronze Age tomb H.22 at Jericho before clearance.

Professor Garstang, and to excavate more of the rich tombs known to lie in the vicinity of the city.'[9] She laid out her trenches with care to concentrate precisely on these problems, using Garstang's earlier work as a guide to those parts of the mound most likely to yield the answers she sought.

The textual tradition may sometimes provide a specific stimulus. When Yadin discovered a fine city gate of the Solomonic period at Hazor he was prompted by I Kings 9:15 to seek comparable gates at Gezer and Megiddo, both sites excavated earlier, but without identification of any such structures.[10] Turning to Macalister's report of 1912 on Gezer, Yadin astutely recognised that a plan captioned 'Maccabean Castle' included part of such a gate missed by the original excavator. Some years after this surmise, American excavators uncovered the whole gate, fully substantiating Yadin's

Plate 11 Tell Masos: aerial view of the excavation of an early Iron Age
settlement.

arguments. Through analysis of the report of American excavations at Megiddo (1925–39) and brief, selective re-excavation, Yadin himself demonstrated that there was indeed a third such Solomonic city gate there, so like those
at Gezer and Hazor as to presuppose a single architectural blueprint in
Solomon's office of works.

Regular application of new methodology to sites previously excavated is
a vital aspect of excavation in Palestine and the strongest argument against
total excavation of any site, even if it were physically and financially possible,
however small. Tell en-Nasbeh (?Mizpah) is the only *tell* so far virtually
cleared. Dever, in writing of the 1964–68 research at Gezer, for instance,

makes clear that the new excavation was made 'with the deliberate intention of getting a carefully dug stratigraphic sequence by which to disentangle and date the fortifications exposed by Macalister.'[11] This same excavation also illustrates how supplementary information may be gleaned from areas supposed to have been completely cleared. The 'High Place' at Gezer, discovered by Macalister in 1902, has had an established, if debatable, place in biblical studies ever since. Both its date, variously placed from the late Chalcolithic to the Iron Age, and its function, have been open to controversy. 'Strategy', writes Dever, 'was dictated by the fact that material was left *in situ* only immediately below the monoliths, where Macalister had not dared to dig.

Therefore we laid out a longitudinal section line, angling slightly to bisect all monoliths on a north/south line. Transverse sections were also laid out against both faces of each monolith. Elaborate scaffolding was erected to hold up the monoliths . . .'[12] In one place, happily of crucial stratigraphic significance, Macalister had left a small area untouched and here it was possible, from pottery sherds sealed beneath a plaster pavement, to provide a date for the 'High Place' at the very end of the Middle Bronze Age, about 1600 BC.

Palestinian archaeological research is now undoubtedly both more problem orientated and more scientifically controlled; but still chance plays a decisive role in its development. This is not only true in the obvious sense, implied by one excavator's slightly resentful remark that 'Our program was to excavate texts but not the one we stumbled on . . .'[13] Significant discoveries are regularly, if randomly, made by following up chance finds of objects revealed by Bedouin, who either bring them direct to excavators in dig camps or sell them to dealers in towns, where they catch the eye of experts. The now famous fourth century Aramaic papyri, from a cave in the Wadi ed-Daliyeh, were first recognised by scholars in Jerusalem when shown to them by a dealer. Bedouin guides subsequently revealed the findspot and controlled excavation by Lapp followed in 1963. Whilst he was at work, a group of peasants arrived seeking employment. One carried a large sack of pottery. Apart from a few Byzantine lamps, it was almost entirely full of pottery of the Early to Middle Bronze Age (Middle Bronze I period), said to have come from a cistern. Lapp followed up the report and discovered not a cistern, but a tomb of the period, forming part of a cemetery at Dhahr Mirzbaneh.

Such initiatives may often involve a waiting game. Between 1960 and 1965 a steadily increasing flow of Early Bronze Age pots began appearing in the antiquities shops of the Old City of Jerusalem, variously said to be from the Hebron area and Qumran. In 1964 reports suggested that the true source was a cemetery just to the south of a large fortified site at Bab edh-Dhra' near the eastern shore of the Dead Sea, facing the Lisan. Subsequent excavation there revealed one of the most important of all Palestinian Early Bronze Age sites.

A particularly good illustration of the evolution of an archaeological project, from exploratory survey through to selective excavation, is provided by Rothenberg's work on the mining region of the Timna valley, opening out of the west side of the Wadi Arabah, north of Eilat-Aqaba.[14] When preliminary exploration began in 1959 some slag heaps had been reported in the area, but no actual ancient copper mines or ore deposits had then been located. Work in the next two years by archaeologists and geologists revealed such deposits and the ancient mines, with the extensive mining camps for those involved in exploiting them. At this point conclusions about the chronology and technology of the mining operations were entirely based on surface observation. The director of the expedition reformulated his aims in 1964, 'to find the actual smelting furnaces and workshops, a good collection of stratified flints and pottery, and to obtain indisputable absolute dates for the Timna industries and sites.' Over the next decade these goals were steadily achieved, with the added discovery of a Late Bronze Age shrine for the Egyptian mining goddess Hathor, from which came votive gifts bearing the names of Egyptian pharoahs – very valuable chronological indicators. In spite of the traditional associations of King Solomon with this mining region, controlled research yielded no evidence that it had been exploited in his reign. Indeed there appeared to have been a gap in use from about the late twelfth century BC to the Roman period.

Notes

1. R. G. Bullard, 'Geological Studies in Field Archaeology', in *Bib. Arch.* 33(1970), pp. 98ff.
2. Cited by G. E. Wright 'A Problem of Ancient Topography : Lachish and Eglon' in *Bib. Arch.* 34 (1971), pp. 76ff.; for another approach see H. J. Franken, 'The Problem of Identification in Biblical Archaeology' *P.E.Q.* (1976), pp. 3ff.; on the complex matter of names see A. Rainey, 'The Toponymics of Eretz-Israel' in *B.A.S.O.R.* 231 (1978), pp. 1ff.
3. W. F. Albright in J. B. Pritchard, *Ancient Near Eastern Texts*, Princeton, 1955, p. 322.
4. See G. E. Kirk, *P.E.Q.* (1938), pp. 211ff.
5. C. L. Woolley, *Dead Towns and Living Men*, London 1932 edition, pp. 275–6.
6. T. L. Thompson, 'Observations on the Bronze Age in Jordan', *Q.D.A.J.* XIX (1974), pp. 63ff.; *The Historicity of the Patriarchal Narratives: The Quest for the Historical Abraham*, Berlin, 1974.
7. K. W. Butzer in W. C. Brice (Ed.) *The Environmental History of the Near and Middle East*, London, 1978.
8. *Hazor: The Rediscovery of a Great Citadel of the Bible*, London, 1975, p. 11.
9. *P.E.Q.* (1952), p. 64.
10. Y. Yadin, *I.E.J.*, 8 (1958), pp. 80–6.
11. *P.E.Q.* (1973), p. 63.
12. Op. cit., p. 69.
13. H. J. Franken in J. Hoftijzer and G. van der Kooij, *Aramaic Texts from Deir 'Alla* London, 1976 p. 3.
14. *Timna: Valley of the Biblical Copper Mines*, London, 1972, p. 22.

George Adam Smith, *The Historical Geography of the Holy Land*, 1st Edition, 1894;
   paperback of final edition, London, 1966. The classic study of the historical
   geography of Palestine. Although the conclusions have naturally been subject to
   revision (see Aharoni below), the descriptions of the landscape are unsurpassed.
Y. Aharoni, *The Land of the Bible: A Historical Geography*, London, 2nd edn., 1979.
   The standard work down to the Exile.
M. Avi-Yonah, *The Holy Land: From the Persian to the Arabian Conquests (536* BC –
   AD *640): A Historical Geography*, Grand Rapids, Michigan, 1966. The most concise
   study of this period.
M. Avi-Yonah (Ed.) *Encyclopedia of Archaeological Excavations in the Holy Land*, 4
   vols, Oxford, 1975–78.
N. Glueck, see the book list for chapter 2.
C. Vita-Finzi, *Archaeological Sites in their Setting*, London, 1978. The pioneer of
   'catchment analysis' in Palestine explains his approach fully.
E. K. Vogel, *Bibliography of Holy Land Sites* offprinted from the *Hebrew Union
   College Annual* XL11 (1971), Cincinnati, 1974.

There is as yet no archaeological atlas of Palestine. It will be provided in due course
by the *Tübinger Atlas des Vorderen Orients* now in preparation. Among numerous
biblical atlases the cheap and easily accessible *Oxford Bible Atlas* (H. G. May (Ed.)
2nd Edition, 1974) pays consideration attention to archaeology. Among a series of
important monographs appearing as part of the Tübingen Atlas the following are
particularly relevant: T. L. Thompson, *The Settlement of Sinai and the Negev in the
Bronze Age, The Settlement of Palestine in the Bronze Age*, Wiesbaden, 1975 and 1979.

4

Excavation

The archaeological landscape of Palestine, as we have seen, is dominated by mounds (*tells*) (Plates 3,5,7). They have been the primary subject of excavation there since the last decade of the nineteenth century and must necessarily monopolise this chapter. But whether it be a mound or a low level settlement site (Plates 11,12), a cave or a cemetery that is under investigation, the basic principles of excavation remain the same.

The growth of a *tell*, if in fact complex, is simply explained. When buildings of mud or mudbrick or stony rubble with plastered walls and roofs collapse, they leave little or nothing to salvage and the remains are merely levelled off and built over. In the course of time through the erosion of wind and water as well as human activity, this accumulating debris forms a mound. Why, it might well be asked, did people choose to build over old houses rather than select new sites on level ground? Two reasons were probably most decisive. Agricultural land, vital for survival in Palestine, always began close to a settlement leaving little room for expansion. More often than not the town or village would also have been fortified and any lateral expansion beyond the walls would have involved costly modification to the defences. Only in the Hellenistic and Roman periods did circumstances change significantly. Then the small mound top no longer sufficed. It was abandoned and the population moved to more spacious areas nearby, often, as at Jericho, taking the ancient name with them to the new site. The earliest occupation levels of the larger *tells* may lie well below the modern land surface, particularly in river valleys where recurrent flooding and deposits of silt progressively raised the surrounding land to keep pace with the accumulation of man made refuse forming the mound.

All archaeological excavation depends on the fact that the sequence of remains in such *tells* may be detected and recorded by digging trenches into them. Stratigraphy, observing the layers of debris in the growth of the mound, enables changes in architecture and domestic equipment, with all the other durable remains of human, animal and plant life, to be placed in order of time and related to observed interruptions or major modifications in the settlement's history. Although the excavation of a *tell* is regularly

Plate 12 Work in progress during the 1970s on the excavation of a major Edomite
settlement of the eighth and seventh centuries BC at Tawilan in Jordan.

compared to stripping the layers off a cake, the analogy is not really appropriate. In a mound the layers are endlessly complex, never level, continuous,
or homogeneous. As any visitor to a modern Near Eastern town or village
will be well aware, buildings, often those side by side in the same street,
grow, decay and are repaired or rebuilt at different rates and at different
times.

If the anatomies of mounds naturally vary, there are certain constants,
only a few of which may be highlighted here by way of illustration. Destruction by fire is one of the most evident phenomena encountered by the
excavator, 'Masonry, consolidated into a chalky white mass streaked with
red, had flowed in a liquid stream over the burnt road surface and lower
wall, below which were piled charred heaps of timber.'[1] More elusive, but
no less significant, are any signs of a break in occupation usually marked by

the growth of turf levels or new ground surfaces over abandoned ruins. Deep shafts for burials or pits for rubbish or storage are cut down into earlier levels of occupational debris, disturbing and confusing them, as well as carrying later objects down amongst earlier ones. Burrowing mammals penetrate deep into the soft soil formed by decayed mudbrick and human occupation rubbish, mixing layers and objects in a bewildering way. Foundations set into deep trenches, especially those for the massive stone public buildings of the Hellenistic and Roman period, were sunk far down into earlier levels. In their turn they were often cut about by later robber trenches used to recover the stone of the foundation courses when the buildings had fallen into decay or disuse. All such deep digging in antiquity complicates the excavator's task of unravelling the stages in a mound's growth. Above all earthquake action, as in the Jordan valley, creates stratigraphic displacements of extraordinary complexity.

In the simplest terms *tell* excavation involves two procedures: deep, vertical cuts, which are designed to reveal the sequence of occupation on the site as economically and directly as possible, and broad, horizontal exposures, which serve to reveal substantial building complexes in specific periods. The art of *tell* excavation rests in the satisfactory combination of the two, to achieve the maximum information with minimum expenditure. The vertical trench is more often than not the crucial preliminary. It should be said at once that step cuttings down the side of a mound, a popular way of making vertical explorations, need careful analysis. Tip lines of debris may be particularly complex towards the edge of a mound, where they will have been most exposed to earth movement and erosion.

With this basic sequence as a guide, excavation may proceed through selected broad cuttings and deep trenches. The area of the *tell* is surveyed, a grid established, and the excavation areas laid out within it. No one would now attempt, even were it financially possible, the plan envisaged at Megiddo in the 1920s and 1930s of stripping away the entire mound, layer by layer from top to bottom. As we have already observed in the previous chapter opportunity must be left for future generations to use new methods on the major *tells*. But whatever the method of trenching, and it will inevitably vary from mound to mound, the same basic principle of excavation applies. Debris must be removed with the greatest care, layer by layer, according to the natural lines of deposit, not by arbitrary depths.

This procedure is far more difficult than it may sound, fully employing both hand and eye. It is the single most important reason why mechanical aids to excavation have little or no place in field archaeology. In Palestine, where the sun may so rapidly bake the exposed sides of a trench as they are revealed, the sharpest of eyes or the most sensitive management of a trowel or pick point may be needed to recognise the vital changes of colour or consistency distinguishing one layer from another. The sides of a trench or wide cutting may be dampened from time to time to bring out colour variations, or observed by varying light through the day. But whatever the means, the digger must be constantly observing and interrogating them as he goes down. Are the lines seen in his trench sides rubbish tips or floor levels? Are they disturbed and, if so, why? Are there any indications of destruction by fire or of a break in occupation marked by layers of windblown sand or by the debris of turf or other vegetation sealing in ruined buildings? Exactly how does the debris relate to the floor or foundation levels of the building under excavation? And so the questions run on.

The purpose of this meticulous attention to the natural bedlines of the debris that constitute the mound is simple, but fundamental: the dating of structures will depend ultimately on the study of the objects associated with them. So it is vital that the exact interrelationships of objects, walls and debris should always be clearly defined and recorded. They may well not all be understood at the time of excavation, but scrupulous recording will ensure, as far as is possible, that all basic information is available for later assessment in a wider context.

It is often hard for the layman to appreciate how little is indicated chronologically by the absolute depth of an object from the surface, or any arbitrarily fixed datum line; both accepted ways of recording objects in the pioneering days of archaeology. If a floor slopes, as most do on Palestinian excavations, an object found at one side contemporary with an object at the other may be vertically separated from it by a quarter of a metre or more. A pit cut down from above might bring to a point between them on the floor an object hundreds of years younger. Such confusions are commonplace in excavations conducted without proper attention to the natural sequence of layers, and the numerous intrusions which always distort them. Only if the levels above the floor have been carefully observed, and lifted with the objects recorded in their appropriate relationship to debris (with the pit cleared separately) will the correct chronological situation emerge. Debris, moreover, accumulates very variably in a mound. An object found one metre below another in an area of slow accumulation may be hundreds of years earlier, whilst in a case of sudden destruction two sherds, separated vertically by a metre of debris, can be from the same pot.

The key to a town's history is most easily established by cutting trenches through its defences in various places and by giving detailed attention to at least one gateway. The gateway at Tell ed-Duweir (Lachish), already referred to (p. 39), may serve as an example. The British excavators (1932–8) studied the superimposed Iron Age gates in area G of the excavations on the *tell*,

Plate 13   Aphek: Late Bronze Age courtyard with overlying post-palace level and ash layers of the eleventh century.

with their related fortification walls and roadways.[2] The earlier inner city gate of levels IV–III was a massive gatehouse with four sets of piers flanking the passage way. Though modified at various times, it was only destroyed by fire once at the end of level III. The outer pair of piers was covered by the superimposed level II city gate and fortification wall. There was indication of occupation over the ruins of the level III gateway, before that of II was built, suggesting an interval when this part of Tell ed-Duweir was unfortified. The city wall, gate and related roads of level II, in which two phases were detected, were all destroyed by fire. The latest city gate, that of level I, was of the Persian period.

Miss Tufnell's absolute dating of these various periods in her publication of the British excavations in 1953 met with severe and authoritative criticism. The debate had such important implications for other sites in Palestine in the later eighth and seventh centuries BC, that when an Israeli expedition returned to dig et Tell ed-Duweir in 1973 it naturally gave priority to area G.[3] Very careful re-investigation produced results which the Israeli scholars believe to be entirely consonant with Miss Tufnell's position, not that of her critics. The city known as III had indeed been that sacked by the Assyrian King Sennacherib in 701 BC (Plate 14), not as many had earlier argued the city attacked by the Babylonians in 597 BC at the time of the fall of Jerusalem. City II was that taken by Nebuchadnezzar in 587/6 BC. In short, remains once attributed by many reputable scholars to a decade had been shown, as Miss Tufnell had originally proposed, to stretch across three generations in the seventh century BC, with substantial repercussions on the chronological assessment of the pottery of Judah and beyond.

Chronology is only the skeleton of history; economic, social and religious life are its flesh and blood. Recovery of representative parts of a town plan in various periods is the most usual way of pursuing them in the archaeological record. Whereas the contours of a mound will usually reveal the location of the defensive system and in some cases the most probable position of the gateways, other public buildings are not similarly defined on the surface. It is only on those relatively small sites where there is no heavy overburden of later levels that sufficient may be revealed of towns for their functional aspects to be fully studied. This has proved possible at Arad, one of the earliest towns in Palestine established at the outset of the Bronze Age, and not far away at Beersheba for the later Iron Age levels.[4] Here, within a circuit of walls, are now revealed the main elements in the layout of a town with its private houses, its store-houses, its water system, roads, and what may be a shrine, destroyed in the later eighth or seventh century BC. Where such overall exposures are not feasible, the excavator must explore with test trenches, exploiting first whatever clues the form of surface of the *tell* offers

Plate 14   Sculptured relief from the Assyrian royal palace at Nineveh in Iraq
showing King Sennacherib, enthroned, receiving the surrender of
Lachish (Tell ed-Duweir), *c*. 701 BC.

for the location of a fortified acropolis or a temple complex, and then opening
up those areas revealed by his trial trenches as most suitable for exploration
of urban complexes.

At this point some attempt must be made to describe for the layman the
actual daily routine of digging on a Palestinian site, since the discipline of
archaeology as applied there will not otherwise be fully understood. The
simplest and most direct approach is to glimpse briefly the work of an
average site supervisor, the junior officer of the archaeological army, responsible for a 10 metre square. Skilled and energetic as an excavation
director may be, the ultimate success of his enterprise very much depends
on the diligence, good sense and recording skills of his site supervisors.
Where labourers rather than students are used each one will have in his
charge a team of local workmen, consisting maybe of one skilled pickman,
two shovellers and half-a-dozen basket boys to take away the earth, when no
mechanical aids for this are available. The supervisor's basic duties are
briefly stated, though by no means so easily executed. He must supervise
the peeling off, along their natural bed lines, of the layers of debris in his
square. He carefully observes, and records fully as he goes along, calling to
his assistance the expedition's photographer, architect, draughtsman or con-
servator when necessary. Through differing colours and textures he must
distinguish the different layers as he goes down, cleaning off each, however

irregularly laid, until he encounters change. In archaeology clean excavation is the main road to accuracy. This process is repeated, usually until a floor level or comparable structural feature is encountered. In the face of any novelty or uncertainty he must stop work, or move his workmen elsewhere, for careful investigation and possible consultation with the director.

If the layman is to appreciate the innate difficulties of this work, he must bear certain relatively obvious but easily overlooked points in mind. Because of the very nature of the work, the excavator is always encountering things in reverse: he will find the debris from a building and its occupation before he encounters its foundation trenches. He is therefore obliged to dig in such a way, perhaps taking one quadrant of his square down slightly in advance of others, as to be able to anticipate as far as he may, what is likely to be uncovered next. A site-supervisor is also, in his small square, generally dealing only with a fragment of a complex horizontal situation. Usually he will only have part of a building in his square, so he must liaise regularly with colleagues excavating squares adjacent to his own. In another important sense he is only handling part of a situation. It is only the two-dimensional ruins of an originally three-dimensional structure that he has before him. In this respect even the most rudimentary knowledge of building construction and collapse is of use to him. This may often most pleasantly and instructively be gleaned by careful observation of modern villages adjacent to the site. In many parts of Palestine, though concrete has transformed so much recently, more traditional ways of building in stone, mudbrick or dried mud still survive.

My account of the Wheeler-Kenyon method in chapter 2 indicated that the key to relationships between walls and debris in an excavation was the sequence revealed in the sides of the trenches, known as *sections* (confusingly used also to describe the drawings of them) or as *baulks*, particularly when they are the intervals between excavated squares in a grid. It is here that the site supervisor and the director have the running guide to what has been excavated in his square. Changes in debris layers, intrusions such as pits, and other features will be revealed there. If part of a structure is being cleared, cross-baulks or small sections against each wall are left so that all connections of wall and debris may be checked. To find a wall and follow it by clearing away the debris on each side, so that it stands free along its whole length, might seem an obvious way to excavate to a laymen, as indeed it did to many pioneer archaeologists. Nothing could be more disastrous, for in doing this the crucial interconnections of the wall and its adjacent debris are destroyed beyond recovery.

As it is only through the recorded sections that the sequence on a site is demonstrable after the excavation is over, it is vital that they should be drawn accurately and regularly on site, not afterwards from photographs, rough sketches or, worst of all, reconstructed from the theodolite levels. It is a cliché to say that archaeological excavation is destruction; but no responsible archaeologist can forget that at the end of the day only his photographs, plans, drawings and records will remain to describe the levels he has cut through. Sections are usually drawn as convenient, and then extended downwards as digging proceeds. The small cross-baulks used in uncovering building foundations will be more regularly drawn, so that the baulk itself can be dismantled to allow for clearer revelation of ground plans. The careful removal of such baulks is an important check on the accuracy of interpretations made through 'reading' the section. A master section for a wide area will eventually be compiled from the smaller section drawings, after direct consultations among site-supervisors, director, and the site architect or surveyor.

Our imaginary site-supervisor, as well as checking the stratigraphy, labelling his sections as the layers are revealed, and writing up his records of them, has also been busy labelling his small finds. Every basket of pottery sherds, very numerous in Palestinian excavations, must contain labels clearly identifying the excavation square whence they came and the layer of debris within that square. Each object is similarly labelled and separately bagged or boxed, with some kind of running record kept in the site-supervisor's notebook. All this material is sorted, cleaned or conserved and properly registered for study by staff at the base camp. Although the site-supervisor will not usually be expected to have a specialist knowledge of small finds, the more he knows, particularly about pottery, the better. As it is largely through the pottery that his debris layers will ultimately be dated, he may be able to identify crucial variations on the spot, if he has discussed his pottery daily, after it has been washed and sorted, with the responsible specialists. Site-supervisors are also increasingly called upon to co-operate with specialists using sieving and water flotation techniques to retrieve seed remains, as well as tiny objects or fragments not easily deteced by eye. Such methods of retrieval have had spectacular results, revealing how much hand and eye alone can miss. In periods when ostraca (inscriptions on sherds) may be expected all sherds should be dipped in water and scrutinised before being sent for the usual thorough washing.

With his excavation over the director is left with the plans, the sections, the field notebooks, the photographs, and the small finds, some processed on the spot, many still to be properly examined. In a very real sense the major part of his task is still before him. It is no exaggeration to say that

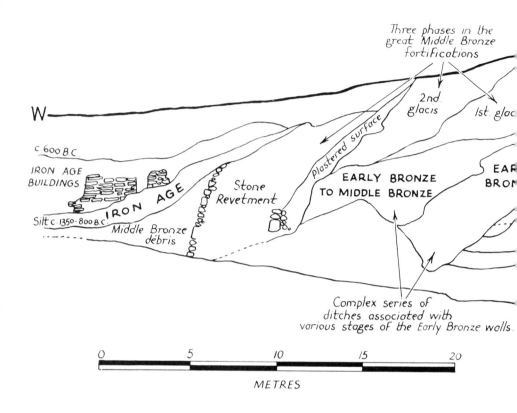

Figure 4   Diagrammatic drawing of the main section (trench 1) at Jericho as excavated by Kathleen Kenyon. (Original drawing simplified with the assistance of Kathleen Kenyon, 1962.)

each day of excavation may require months of study to present the information obtained for proper publication; that is why so few excavations have been fully published.

The first task is to establish, through the sections and plans drawn in the field, the sequence and structures in each trench. Each will be phased, with plans drawn of buildings phase by phase, and small finds sorted into the appropriate phase. Then the phasing of each trench must be correlated across the *tell*. This is a very complex operation, the more so if there is no structural link between the various trenches.

Without such links it is the small finds, predominantly the pottery, which

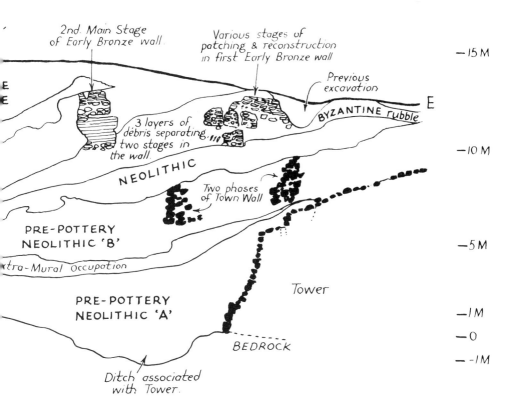

are used to provide link-ups between widely scattered areas, matching assemblages of objects like with like. This will naturally have to wait for full processing of the small finds (see chapter 6). When this evidence is all assembled and integrated, the main periods of occupation on the tell may finally be defined, with the phases from the individual units of the excavation fitted into it.[5]

This highly selective account of excavation in Palestine has necessarily concentrated on the ubiquitous *tell*; but there is little in the general principles considered that does not equally well apply to any site under excavation. The second most common type of excavated site after settlements are cemeteries, which provide one significant problem of their own. Here there is usually little or no vertical stratigraphy through which to order the graves in a time sequence. If circumstances permit the cemetery will be excavated by a grid of squares, allowing control across the whole of it, to establish where possible, through the relative position of burials, whether it was used at different times. Each grave is carefully plotted with its skeleton and grave furnishings and drawn in detail. The time sequence may have to be established through statistical analysis of the objects in the graves. Such a method was used for the Middle Bronze Age tombs at Jericho. These were divided up into five successive groups through studying the first appearance, maximum frequency and disappearance of specific pottery types.[6] Each end of the series could then be tied in with the pottery sequence from the adjacent *tell*. The presence in the tombs of Egyptian scarab-seals allowed for some broad correlation with a historic chronology, and that will be the primary concern of the next chapter.

Notes

1. O. Tufnell, *Lachish* III, London, 1953, p. 57, describing the Babylonian destruction in 587/6 BC.
2. Op. cit., pp. 93ff.
3. D. Ussishkin, *Tel Aviv* 4 (1977), pp. 28ff.; also 'Lachish' in *Encyclopedia of Archeological Excavations in the Holy Land*, Vol. III; *Tel Aviv* 5 (1978), pp. 1ff.
4. For summaries of both these excavations see the *Encyclopaedia*.
5. See K. M. Kenyon, 'An Essay on Archaeological Technique: The Publication of Results from the Excavation of a Tell', *Harvard Theological Review* 64 (1971), pp. 271ff.
6. K. M. Kenyon, *Jericho* I, London, 1960 *Jericho* II, London, 1965, pp. 167ff.

Recommended Reading

The articles and books listed on p. 35 are also very relevant here. Two further books, which are primarily concerned with the Near East outside Palestine, offer much relevant information,

Seton Lloyd, *Mounds of the Near East*, Edinburgh, 1963. This survey of excavation and survey techniques contains some cogent criticisms of the Wheeler-Kenyon method.

Leonard Woolley, *Digging up the Past*, London 1930; 2nd edition 1954. This short book is a vivid introduction to Near Eastern field archaeology by one of its great exponents; its date of publication should, however, be borne in mind by the reader.

The increasing number of books on archaeological excavation techniques very rarely, if ever, make specific reference to Palestine; the following three are representative,

John Alexander, *The Directing of Archaeological Excavations*, London, 1970.

P. A. Barker, *Techniques of Archaeological Excavation*, London, 1977; see particularly his chapter on the interpretation of stratigraphy.

Graham Webster, *Practical Archaeology*, London, 2nd revised edition, 1974.

But see particularly,

W. G. Dever and H. D. Lance (Eds.), *A Manual of Field Excavation – Handbook for Field Archaeologists*, Hebrew Union College – Jewish Institute of Religion, Jerusalem, 1978.

5

After Excavation: Establishing time-scales

One of the first problems facing the archaeologist when he moves from excavation to interpretation is the fundamental question of dating. Only if he can set his finds into some chronological framework will he be able to bring order out of chaos and construct a narrative into which his finds may be properly integrated. Until the later part of the nineteenth century all historical chronology for Palestine, as for the rest of the world was firmly based on the genealogies given in the Old Testament. In his *Annales Veteris et Novi Testamenti* James Ussher (1581–1656), Archbishop of Armagh, had summarised in Latin the history of the world from the creation, placed in 4004 BC, to the dispersion of the Jews under Vespasian. For centuries his chronology was printed in the Authorized Version of the Bible. Now that the precision of this seventeenth century divine in dating the creation is treated as a joke, it is very difficult to appreciate the enormous intellectual revolution which, in the nineteenth century, transformed man's conception of the antiquity of the world in which he lived.

Lyell's *Principles of Geology*, published between 1830–33, presented the concept of extended time in geology. He argued that the agencies forming geological strata had always proceeded at a uniform rate comparable with similar modern conditions of deposit; in short, the natural world must be more than 6000 years old. It followed that the human bones and artefacts already recognised under thick layers of earth or stalagmite must have been deposited there very long ago. A generation later, Darwin's two major works, *On the Origin of Species by Means of Natural Section* (1859) and *The Descent of Man* (1871), provided the crucial theory to explain why the natural world and man were a continuous not an instant creation, the product of a very long evolutionary process which is still being charted and dated.

Relative chronology

What follows, as we have seen in the previous chapter, from a carefully controlled excavation is only a sequence, a relative chronology, in which layer A is before layer B, B before C, and so on; the contents of A, allowing for intrusions, earlier than the contents of B. The precise ages and the lengths of time involved remain a mystery. Before steps can be taken to establish them, the archaeological data must be broadly classified.

A generation earlier than the great intellectual debates on the age of man and his artefacts in the middle of the last century, Danish antiquarians had established a system for classifying objects that still endures, though much modified and refined. Originally conceived through the study of museum collections, it was subsequently confirmed by excavations. This system proposed a division into the 'three ages' of Stone, Bronze and Iron. It is a highly effective method for establishing a relative chronology enduring still in Palestinian archaeology, for again there is no indication of precise timescales. The Stone Age, which is not our concern here, embraces with many sub-divisions the Old or Palaeolithic and the New or Neolithic, broken down further by the presence or absence of pottery (Pre-pottery or Aceramic Neolithic). A transitional Chalcolithic phase to mark the earliest use of metal in the fourth millennium BC, survives in Palestinian terminology though now often dropped elsewhere. In these early periods various local cultural terminologies (Tahunian; Ghassulian) are also used.

The so-called Bronze Age, though copper long remained the predominant base metal, is divided into three major phases, Early, Middle and Late, covering the third and second millennia BC. The Early Bronze Age (c. 3300–2300 BC) is now usually subdivided into four divisions, I, II, III, IV, broken down further by some authorities into A and B phases. The Middle Bronze Age opens with a phase variously termed Intermediate Early to Middle Bronze (Kenyon) or Middle Bronze I (Albright). It is consequently necessary to remember that the use of the subdivisions IIA, IIB and IIC will vary slightly as to which initial terminology has been adopted by a particular writer. The period runs from about 2300–1550 BC. The Late Bronze Age, again variously subdivided, covers the next three centuries. The Iron Age, taken to extend down from 1200 BC to the Persian supremacy about 540 BC, is divided again in I and II subdivided a, b, c with scholars differing over the precise dating of the subdivisions. The attribution of the various levels of different *tells* to particular subphases of these major divisions is a matter of constant study and reappraisal, constantly stimulated by freshly excavated evidence (see table on p.10).

Owing to the random and unpredictable rate of debris accumulation in a *tell* only in the most exceptional circumstances will it provide any direct indication of the rate of passing time. In Early Iron Age Deir 'Alla, for instance, the courtyards had been recurrently covered with layers of reeds reinforced with clay in the 'first period' (phases A-D).[1] About forty such

Plate 15 Tell el-Hesi: first excavated by Petrie in 1890, viewed from the south-west during the American excavations in 1977. Several of the excavated squares can be seen as dark areas on the lower slopes of the acropolis.

superimposed reed pavings were detected in the main east-west section across the whole excavated area. It was suggested that these might represent a regular, possibly annual, deposit. Two isolated C14 datings (see pp. 77f.) do not destroy this hypothesis. A date determination on charcoal from a roof beam of the last Bronze Age shrine, the destruction of which coincided with the beginning of phase A, was 1180 ± 60 bc (Groningen, no. 4553). A test on a sample from an ash deposit marking the end of phase D gave 1190 ± 50 bc (Groningen, no. 4749). These indicate a short period of time for the 'first period'. The tentative character of any chronological conclusions to be drawn from so rare a sequence as these reed pavings only serves to emphasise the fallibility of time-scales based on the evidence of debris accumulation rates.

The direct application of a geological clue to the relative dating of levels on different sites in Palestine and Syria has only once been attempted systematically. In 1948 C.F.A. Schaeffer published his monumental *Strati-*

graphie Comparée et Chronologie de l'Asie Occidentale (IIIe et IIe millénaires).
Here he sought to identify the results of earthquake action on a number of
sites in the Near East occupied in the Bronze Age and thus correlate destruction levels on many *tells*. The arguments did not carry conviction. The
basic hypothesis rested on the seismologically unacceptable assumption that
earthquake shocks will be felt simultaneously, and with comparable force,
over a wide area. To sustain his case the author was also soon involved in
questionable identifications of earthquake damage on various sites where the
original excavators had given more routine explanations for the destruction.
Earthquake damage may certainly be identified on archaeological sites, especially in the Jordan valley, but it is evidence that has to be used with
circumspection in chronological arguments. De Vaux attributed the end of
period Ib in the building at Qumran, close to the caves whence came the
Dead Sea Scrolls, to the earthquake of 31 BC, reported by the Jewish
historian Josephus.[2] Some authorities have sought other explanations for the

71

faults de Vaux found in the cisterns at Qumran, which he attributed to earthquake damage. The Qumran building is on geotechnically unstable Lisan Marl, where seepage and percolation might undermine structures.

Absolute chronology

In Palestinian archaeology from the Early Bronze Age onwards transposing relative to absolute chronologies, in years BC/AD, has never been quite so complex a problem as such correlations often are elsewhere. When Petrie excavated Tell el-Hesi in 1890 he was able to use immediately, if only in a rudimentary way, the primary guiding light when digging in regions fresh to archaeology: the principle of cross-dating. This rests very simply on the recognition, in the new area, of actual imports from a region whose absolute chronology is already known. In this case it was Egypt, where Petrie had already undertaken a number of excavations. 'Thus . . . ,' he wrote, 'we must wait till we find objects from other countries of known age, intermixed with those as yet unclassified, in order to spell out the archaeology of a fresh country . . . The materials of known age proved to be scanty in my work; a few pieces of pottery were all I had to rely on. To anyone unfamiliar with such evidences this might seem a slender basis for the mapping out of a history; yet I had full confidence in it. And now that far longer and heavier excavations have been carried on there (i.e. at Tell el-Hesi) by Mr. Bliss, some absolutely dated objects from Egypt, bearing the king's names, and others which we can date by known examples, have amply confirmed the general age to which I had assigned the strata of ruins.'[3]

Egyptian dynastic chronology

Egyptian historical chronology, which begins about 3100 BC, is based by modern scholars on the arrangement of rulers into approximate family groups, known as dynasties, used by the Graeco-Egyptian priest, Manetho, in preparing a history of Egypt in the early third century BC. His dynastic lists have only survived in the abridged versions of the Christian historians, Africanus (early third century AD), Eusebius (early fourth century AD) and a much later compiler known as Syncellus (c. AD 800). Other parts of Manetho's history are preserved in the work of the Jewish historian Josephus (first century AD). For convenience these dynasties have been grouped into blocks: Old Kingdom (1st–VIth dynasties, c. 3100–2181 BC); Middle Kingdom (XIth–XIIth, c. 2133–1786 BC); New Kingdom (XVIIIth–XXth, c. 1567–1085 BC), and the Late Period XXVI–XXXI, c. 664–330 BC), which ends with the Greek conquest opening the Ptolemaic period. The intervals of anarchy, foreign invasion and general political disruption are arbitrarily termed Intermediate periods: the First (VIIth–Xth dynasies, *c.* 2181–2040 BC, overlapping dynasty XI); the Second (XIIIth–XVIIth, *c.* 1786–1567 BC) and the Third (XXIst–XXVth, *c.* 1085–664 BC). It is during these periods that the overlapping of dynasties provides particular chronological difficulties and it may turn out that they were shorter than is at present assumed.

Virtually nothing has survived of the ancient sources available to Manetho. Only two documents, the 'Royal Canon' of Turin compiled in the reign of Ramses II (*c.* 1290–1223 BC) and the much earlier 'Palermo Stone' with related fragments inscribed during the Vth dynasty (*c.* 2490–2340 BC), illustrate the kind of ancient annals he might have used. Three other lists, of kings' names only, inscribed on monuments at Abydos, Saqqara and Karnak during the New Kingdom (*c.* 1567–1085 BC), though selective, provide valuable comparative evidence. These may be supplemented in some cases by contemporary historical records, by biographical inscriptions, and by literary works with relevant historical information. These lists of king's names in the order of their succession provide only a relative chronology. The establishment of an absolute chronology in regnal years is a complex process. Although some ancient records give the length of reigns, the uneven character of the surviving evidence and the possibility of partly contemporaneous, rather than consecutive, dynasties, means that dates before about 1550 BC may only be approximate, and even thereafter there may be a margin of decades in certain cases. Astronomical observations provide crucial, if isolated, fixed points.

The Egyptian Civil Calendar (they also used two lunar religious ones) consisted of 12 months of 30 days each, to which were added five days to complete a 365-day year. Each period of 12 months was divided into 3 seasons, the year beginning in the season of Inundation. In the ideal year the first day of the year coincided with the first day on which the dog-star Sirius could be seen on the eastern horizon just before the rising of the sun (i.e. it rose heliacally), about 19 or 20 July in our calendar. The Egyptians of the dynastic period never introduced a leap year, so New Year's Day advanced by one whole day in relation to the natural year in every period of four years. Consequently New Year's Day and the day on which Sirius rose heliacally coincided for no more than four years in every period of about 1460 years (4 x 365). This is the Sothic Cycle regularly referred to in reference books.

As it is known from Roman sources that New Year's Day in AD 139 coincided with the rise of Sirius heliacally it may be calculated that this had happened previously, in the historic period, in 1322 and 2782 BC, or astronomically more precisely in 1314 and 2770 BC. Including the Roman record there are seven ancient Egyptian documents which give Sothic dates, but only two yield results in terms of regnal years. These allow us to calculate that the ninth regnal year of Amenophis I of the XVIIIth dynasty was in the range 1544–1537 BC and that year seven of the earlier Sesostris III, of the XIIth dynasty, was 1872 BC.[4] Even so there is a possibility that these so-called Sothic dates may be 25 years or so too early, if the point of observation was Thebes and not the region of Memphis-Heliopolis, further north, as is commonly assumed.

Although ancient Egyptian chronology is often referred to as 'fixed', it will be apparent that this is a relative term. In so far as ancient historic chronologies go, before those of Greece and Rome, it is indeed well-established and for most archaeological purposes the margins of error are insignificant. But they most certainly exist, and not only in the third millennium BC. Regular minor modifications in Egyptian historic chronology in the New Kingdom and later have significant repercussions on the absolute chronology of Palestine in the time of the Judges and the Monarchy. Palestinian chronology at this time, and to a lesser extent earlier, is fortunate in having another historic chronology, that of ancient Mesopotamia (Assyria and Babylonia), with which it may be linked. Distance, and less intense commercial and diplomatic contact, made relations between Palestine and Mesopotamia less common than with Egypt. But in certain periods, notably in the later Middle Bronze Age (1750–1550 BC), and during the Assyrian and Babylonian invasions of Iron Age IIb-c (about 800–580 BC), the association was important.

Mesopotamian historic chronology

The foundations of modern knowledge of Mesopotamian absolute chronology were laid by a Greek astronomer Ptolemy, living in Alexandria in Egypt in the second century AD. In his *System of Mathematics*, known as the *Almagest* or 'great work', he tells us that he had to hand records of lunar eclipses at Babylon back to the reign of King Nabonassar (*c.* 747–734 BC). These included an eclipse about 720 BC under a king named in Greek as Mardokempados (Marduk-apla-iddina = Merodach-Baladan II). Ptolemy's list of the kings of Babylon with their regnal years was not included in the *Almagest*, but has been preserved in the writings of the fourth century Alexandrian scholar Theon. He gives the regnal years of rulers at Babylon from Nabonassar down to Alexander the Great and his successors. Astronomical observations recorded on baked clay tablets found at Babylon provide evidence for an independent check on the accuracy of Ptolemy and

Plate 16   The 'Weld-Blundell' prism inscribed with the most important surviving copy of the Sumerian King List from before the 'Flood' to about 1817 BC; 20 cm high.

Theon's absolute chronology back to the eighth century BC.

As certain kings of Assyria also claimed authority over Babylon at this time, they appear in Theon's list, allowing it to be correlated with the much fuller surviving Assyrian King–lists, inscribed on clay tablets, running back to the fourteenth century BC. A solar eclipse recorded for the month of *Sivan* (May–June) in the tenth year of the Assyrian king Ashur-Dan II is identified with the astronomically computed eclipse of 15 June, 763 BC. Before the fourteenth century BC the margin of error in absolute chronology in Mesopotamia rises appreciably. One problem in particular is critical and must be mentioned here as it is very relevant to correlations with Palestine in the later Middle Bronze Age. The date of the First Dynasty of Babylon, to which the famous King Hammurabi belonged, still floats over a period of at least 120 years.

According to current understanding the end of this dynasty might be either in 1650, 1594, 1586 or 1530 BC. These intervals are governed by the primary surviving astronomical evidence. From the reign of King Ammi-saduqa, the tenth and penultimate ruler of this dynasty, have survived records of the first and last visibility of Venus as morning and evening star for 21 years of his reign. This king began his reign 52 years before the end of the dynasty. The records only survive in late, corrupt copies, but astronomical calculations have corrected them where necesary.[5] The dates of the first and last appearances of Venus in the intercalated Babylonian lunar calendar virtually repeat every 56 ± 8 years. With the help of the Venus Observations, and supplementary archaeological and historical evidence from a wide variety of sources, the majority of scholars have increasingly come to accept the 'Middle Chronology', ending the First Dynasty of Babylon about 1595 BC and thereby dating Hammurabi *c.* 1792–1750 BC. This is the system adopted for the revised *Cambridge Ancient History*. Students of Palestinian archaeology need to be aware that Albright always argued for a lower chronology which sets the end of the dynasty at about 1530 BC. As documents from the great palace at Mari on the Euphrates in modern Syria reveal that Hammurabi was a contemporary of King Shamshi-Adad I of Assyria, the records of Assyria and Babylonia may thereby be linked.

King-lists, year-names and occasional synchronisms allow for a plausible reconstruction of absolute chronology back another five hundred years or so from the beginning of the First Dynasty, on the Middle Chronology about 1890 BC, to the time of the earliest kings in south Mesopotamia (Sumer) for whom contemporary inscriptions have survived. A crucial source in this reconstruction is an inscribed baked clay prism, named after its first modern owner Weld-Blundell, giving the best surviving copy of the Sumerian King-list (Plate 16). This remarkable document extends back to the mythological rulers of Sumer before the 'flood' and runs down to the eleventh year of King Sinmagir of the city of Isin about 1817 BC. Use of such a list in reconstructing absolute chronologies is hampered by the recording in succession of dynasties that certainly overlapped and the inflated lengths given to the reigns of some rulers. The compilers were more interested in the sequence of events than in the intervals between them. Thus in Sumer, as in Egypt, it is in the third millennium BC that modern scientific aids for establishing absolute chronologies are as vital to the text-aided archaeologist as they are at all times to his text-free colleagues. Carbon-14 dating is still undoubtedly the most important of these for any but the more remote prehistoric periods.

Carbon-14 dating

About 1946 Professor W.F. Libby of Chicago University discovered an ageing process inherent in organic materials, outstandingly for archaeology, charcoal and bone, that within certain limits makes it possible to determine the age of samples in years. All living matter contains a small but practically constant proportion of the radioactive isotope of carbon, *Carbon-14* (C^{14}). This is produced by cosmic-ray bombardment of nitrogen atoms in the outer atmosphere. When an animal or a plant dies the radioactive carbon in its tissue ceases to be replenished from the atmosphere. Indeed it disintegrates at a constant rate. After a certain length of time half will have disintegrated radioactively and half will be left in the original radioactive form. This time interval is known as the 'half life' originally determined for radiocarbon ($=C^{14}$) as 5,568 ($\pm$ 30) years. Thus, if measurement of the radioactivity of a sample indicates a quarter of that in a modern sample, then the age of it may be set at two half-lifes or about 11,150 years BP (Before Present).

All radiocarbon dates are published with a plus or minus figure, 1525 $\pm$ 75 BC. This often leads to confusion since it expresses a statistical concept. It does not mean that the statistical uncertainty (commonly referred to as the 'error') is precisely the amount quoted, nor that the proper reading must necessarily be within the limits apparently set. It indicates that the best estimate for the correct value is 1525 BC with a 'standard deviation' of 75 years. This means more specifically that the correct value has a 66% probability of lying within the limits given, i.e. 1525 + 75 to 1525 – 75 BC. It has a 95% probability of lying within the limits of two standard deviations, i.e. 1525 + 150 to 1525 – 150 BC, and a 99.5% probability of lying within three standard deviations. It will be immediately clear that this method is not likely to provide fundamental information for a Palestinian archaeological context where the Egyptian historical chronology may be applied.

Two of the assumptions underlying Libby's development of radiocarbon dating require further comment. First, it was assumed that Carbon-14 has a single, fixed half-life. This view still stands, although laboratory measurement of it has been refined in recent years. The best available estimate of the half-life is now set at 5730±30 years, about 3.4% longer than the previous value established by Libby. Ages calculated on the old 5,568 half-life (in years BP, Before Present, conventionally taken as 1950) may be adjusted through multiplication by 1.03. If the figure to be recalculated is already given in years BC, the adjustment requires multiplication by 1.03 and the addition of 66 years. Clearly, it is very important when quoting Carbon-14 to make clear which half-life value has been used. It has been agreed that dates should be quoted with the old Libby half-life of 5,568 years to avoid confusion. This should be assumed unless otherwise clearly stated.

The second of Libby's assumptions, that the proportion of radiocarbon to ordinary carbon (the common stable isotope, Carbon-12) has remained constant through time, has been shown to be erroneous. The deviations before about 1000 BC are so great as to make significant differences in date determinations. Appreciation of this variation has led to a major re-appraisal of radiocarbon chronologies during the last decade. Since the late 1950s radiocarbon determinations of wood from the very long lived bristle cone pine (sequoia tree) growing in the White Mountains of California, dated independently by counting its annual growth rings, have indicated that the concentration of radiocarbon in the atmosphere, and thus in living things, has varied considerably. It was much higher 6000 years ago than it is now. Using Libby's assumption of constancy dates had been determined that were misleadingly recent. Libby himself had already seen that something was amiss when he realised that radiocarbon determinations for Egyptian samples were consistently too recent by comparison with the local historical chronology. It was to become clear that it was the radiocarbon calendar, not the historical chronology for Egypt, which was in error.

Now, through radiocarbon determinations of tree-ring samples of known date from the bristle cone pine, graphs have been constructed which may be used to convert radiocarbon dates, in radiocarbon years, to true or tree-ring dates in calendar years BC/AD. This calibration process, though still a matter of debate and research, has become a necessary part of Carbon-14 studies. All who use radiocarbon dates need to be aware of it. It is increasingly the convention that bc is written when using simple, uncalibrated radiocarbon dates, and the capitals BC only when the dates are expressed in calendar years after calibration. The situation is made more complex for the non-specialist by the existence of several calibration curves or graphs, each differing slightly in the results given, since much more information on short term Carbon-14 fluctuations is still needed in many areas. It is all the more important then that any use of radiocarbon date determinations should give as many details as possible: what type of material was sampled (charcoal, bone, etc.); what its precise archaeological context was; what the original radiocarbon date (BP) was, with its laboratory code number; which half-life and which calibration curve was used in determining the value in years BC/AD. A typical instance might be,

Lab No.	Sample	Source	5568 Half-Life	5730 Half-Life	MASCA Calibration
P-2299	Charred grain	Ai: Phase V (E.B. IIb) Ref CI 1.286	4200±70 BP	2376±72 bc	2940–20±70 BC

In using radiocarbon dates amateurs and professionals alike all too often ignore the fundamental fact that radiocarbon measurements date the age of the organic tissue of the sample – the time when it originated. It is quite possible that the tissue of a sample from a specific archaeological context might have been biologically dead for several decades or even centuries before ancient man used it, whether in building or for fuel. A distinction between potentially young material, say charred grain, and potentially old material, such as structural timbers, may be crucial. Single dates must always be treated with the greatest caution. As Carbon-14 dating is based on statistical calculations it is always best to examine a range of samples from the same context in order to analyse the spread of the dates. For the present the importance of radiocarbon dating for Palestine is concentrated on the prehistoric periods and the third millennium BC, where the independent historic chronologies are either unavailable or known to be fallible. In a careful review of all the Carbon-14 dates available up to 1976 for the Palestinian Early Bronze Age, Callaway and Weinstein[6] were able to show that they indicated a higher chronology for the beginning of the period (c. 3300 BC) than Albright and other Palestinian archaeologists had previously argued. This was found to be consonant with the latest information available through controlled stratigraphic excavation.

In summary, chronology in Palestine rests on three largely independent foundations. By careful correlation of the relative sequence of levels on each excavated site a composite picture is built up for a specific period across Palestine, as for example,

Early Bronze IIA-B

Ai(Phases IV-V) : Jericho (Phases J-G) : Arad II-I : Bethshan XIV–XII etc.

Then foreign synchronisms are established, if possible through inscriptions, if not through imported seals, pottery or other small objects, which link levels on Palestinian sites to the absolute historic chronologies of Egypt or Mesopotamia. In the example given above, for example, there is a broad correlation between Early Bronze II in Palestine and the Pharoahs of Egypt from Djer, the third ruler of the First Dynasty, to Khasekhem, penultimate ruler of the Second Dynasty. Their dates may be established through Egyptian records, as indicated above (p. 72), and then correlated as appropriate with Carbon-14 datings.[7]

Notes

1. H.J. Franken, *Excavations at Tell Deir 'Alla*, Brill, 1969, pp. 244–5.
2. R. de Vaux, *Archaeology and the Dead Sea Scrolls*, London, 1973, pp. 20ff.; compare I. Karcz and U. Kafri, 'Evaluation of Supposed Archaeoseismic Damage in Israel', *Journal of Archaeological Science* 5 (1978), pp. 237–53.
3. 'The Story of a "Tell" ', a lecture printed by the *P.E.F.*, 1892, p. 6.
4. The Illahun papyrus in question here does not give the name of the pharoah; but other evidence from the same archive of papyri indicates Sesotris III. Calculations of lunar dates recorded in the same documents help to confirm the 1872 dating.
5. However, students should be aware that the recent new critical edition of these texts suggests that they are so corrupt a record as to be of very little use as the base for chronological calculations.
6. 'Radiocarbon Dating of Palestine in the Early Bronze Age', *B.A.S.O.R.* 225 (1977), pp. 1ff.
7. The most recent attempt to reconcile the historical and Carbon-14 chronologies for the Bronze Age, J. Mellaart, 'Egyptian and Near Eastern Chronology : a dilemma?', *Antiquity* 53 (1978), pp. 6ff. is compromised by an unacceptably high interpretation of Egyptian historical chronology, ignoring the Sesostris III Sothic date, and a very debatable treatment of Babylonian historical chronology; see criticisms in *Antiquity*, 55 (1980), pp. 21ff., 128ff.

Recommended Reading

The following books and articles are complementary to the text. They do not include works on complex questions of biblical and Israelite historical chronology which fall outside the range of this book.

T.E. Allibone (Ed.), *The Impact of the Natural Sciences on Archaeology*, Oxford, 1970; especially I.E.S. Edwards on Egypt and A. Sachs on Babylonia and Assyria.

S. Fleming, *Dating in Archaeology : A Guide to Scientific Techniques*, London, 1976.

W.C. Hayes and M.B. Rowton, 'Chronology', *Cambridge Ancient History* I(1), 1970, pp. 173–239.

J.O.D. Johnston, 'The Problems of Radiocarbon Dating', *P.E.Q.* (1973), pp. 13–16, with full bibliography.

R.D. Long, 'Ancient Egyptian Chronology, Radiocarbon Dating and Calibration', *Zeitschrift für Agyptische Sprache und Altertumskunde* 103 (1976), pp. 30–48.

J.W. Michels, *Dating Methods in Archaeology*, New York, 1973.

C. Renfrew, *Before Civilization : the radiocarbon revolution and prehistoric Europe*, London, 1973, for the appendix on radiocarbon dating.

T. Säve-Söderbergh and I.U. Olsen, 'C-14 Dating and Egyptian Chronology' in *Radiocarbon Variations and Absolute Chronologies*, Ed. I.U. Olsen, Nobel Symposium 12, 1970, pp. 35–55. This is a particularly clear exposition of the Egyptian historical chronology.

T. Watkins (Ed.), *Radiocarbon : Calibration and Prehistory*, Edinburgh, 1975.

6

After Excavation:
Structures and small finds

Each settled community in Palestine, represented by an excavated site, was part of a regional unit, and many aspects of its life and that of the wider pattern of settlement to which it belonged cannot be investigated properly through a site by site approach. The proper publication of evidence from each excavation is but a step in a much wider complex of study. The evidence of animal bones, for instance, at any one site must be drawn into much wider geographical and chronological horizons for an intelligent synthesis of animal husbandry. In the same way chemical or petrological analysis of pottery from isolated sites may enable their sources to be identified, but the results will mean very little in economic terms until broad patterns of manufacture and trade are understood. In this chapter, in a very selective way, an attempt has been made to indicate the kind of information to be expected from a study of the 'finds' from an excavation and the means of extracting it. In recent years careful attention to precise stratigraphical digging has been increasingly matched by ever more intensive use of statistical and analytical techniques for extracting maximum information from small finds after their excavation.

Investigation of changing forms through time, whether of buildings or artefacts, the conventional typological approach, remains basic; but a much more extensive range of questions about function, materials and their sources, methods of manufacture, craft traditions, production centres and trade are now asked, and the answers sought with the assistance of scientific methods of analysis. Science has become more than an aid to the excavator, for it may offer alternative methods of investigation yielding fresh types of evidence for reconstructing the past. Much closer attention is paid to proper description, in the appropriate technical terms, to sampling and sorting for statistical presentation, and to the comparisons of assemblages of artefacts rather than of outstanding individual items, often arbitrarily selected. It has made the subject more precise, more complex and all too often, regrettably, more jargon-ridden. Practitioners and laymen alike are now increasingly required to absorb a considerable amount of technical data, if they wish to assess critically the new material emerging in such quantity from the numerous excavations current in Palestine. It needs to be remembered that even the most sophisticated scientific technique does not necessarily yield self-evident truths. The results must be interpreted, as always, as but one aspect of a whole spectrum of evidence.

Structures and functioning communities

The individual household was the social and economic basis of ancient Palestinian settled communities. The comparative study of housing reveals something of regional variations and social status[1], but not always as much as might be hoped of daily life. For this there is a simple explanation. Living quarters were generally on roofs or upper floors; the levels most often found by archaeologists accommodated livestock and storage. Clues to household activity may be gleaned from the objects and fittings of individual houses, but it is comparisons between them on single sites, and from site to site, that yield the most significant information about craft specialisations and domestic industries. All houses may be expected to show some evidence of food procurement, preparation and storage. Economic distinctions emerge only with evidence for potting, textile manufacture, wine or oil production, and organised working of bone, stone or metal. Such activities are recognised most readily when they have grown beyond the requirements of a single household. In most Palestinian settlements of any size each branch of a trade or industry was usually carried on in a particular area, so any substantial craft activity is likely to be concentrated in a group of buildings. Nor is specialist craft equipment as readily recognised in archaeological contexts as might be anticipated.

A seventh century BC weaver's home and workshop excavated at Tell ed-Duweir was identified through a combination of features. 'A stone dying vat set in the floor at the junction of the cobbled surface with the mud floor . . . many clay loom weights . . . fifty-three large, seven medium and nine small loom weights of the "doughnut" shape. The charred remains of a heavy wooden beam set upright at the end of the room suggests the presence of a vertical loom.'[2] Dye-vats and olive presses have more than once been confused in the archaeological literature of Palestine and it was the local labourers at Tell Beit Mirsim who immediately recognised Iron Age dye-vats for Albright.[3] The identification was confirmed and elucidated by comparison with dye-plants active in Hebron at the time of the excavations. Experimental archaeology may be no less instructive than ethnographic analogy in elucidating the remains of ancient industrial installations. In 1970 the Israel Museum reconstructed a late second century AD oil press on the southern slope of the Rehavia valley to study the processes of olive oil manufacture.[4]

Yet there are still cases where neither scientific investigation nor ethnography may confidently resolve problems of this kind. At ʿAin Feshka, on the west shore of the Dead Sea, de Vaux found tanks, channels, pits and basins of the first century AD which had to him the appearance of tannery installations.[5] Analysis of samples taken from them showed no clear sign either of leather or parchment production debris. Other suggestions, fish farming among them, were no better sustained by the available evidence.

The Iron Age winery at el-Jib (Gibeon) well illustrates how it is only a steadily accumulating body of information that yields convincing evidence for industrial installations.[6] This industry at el-Jib was first suggested to the excavators by the recovery of many detached baked clay jar handles inscribed first with the place name 'Gibeon', then the word *gdr*, perhaps meaning a walled vineyard, and finally the name of a person. Excavation revealed storage jars, funnels and stoppers, and features like rockcut grape presses, fermenting tanks, settling basins and storage cellars, which taken together strongly suggested a local wine production centre in the eighth and seventh centuries BC. The jars in which the wine had been stored in rockcut cellars, at a constant temperature of about 65°F (18°C), had a capacity of 9.75 gallons. The excavated cellars, if all in use at the same time, had been capable of holding about 25,000 gallons of wine.

The economic life of a settlement, particularly one of any size, will involve commerce as well as craft installations. This is an elusive subject for textless archaeology, turning more on the evidence of artefacts than of structures. Storehouses alone indicate something of the economic role of a site. They are among the most prominent features of Iron Age towns in Palestine, notably a series at Beersheba,[7] (Plate 6). This excavation went far to confirming Pritchard's suggestion that the buildings found at Megiddo in the 1930s, and long famous as 'King Solomon's Stables', were much more likely to have been storehouses. Reassessments of their stratigraphical position and related pottery had placed them in the Omride dynasty before Pritchard's close analysis of their architectural features left little reason to see them as stables. This is an instructive example of the hazards of resting an open archaeological case too firmly on a special reading of scattered textual allusions. Too much had been made from associating references to Solomon's building at Megiddo (Kings 9:15) with accounts of his chariot cities and his involvement in the trading of horses and chariots (1 Kings 9:19, 10:26–29).

Major buildings for public administration and religious life normally dominate a settlement by setting and size, as well as revealing their character in a general way in their ground plans. Understanding them as functioning institutions will largely elude the archaeologist unless he finds archives of tablets, like those which have given various Bronze Age sites in Syria, such

Plate 17   *Left*: seated bronze statuette of a Canaanite god; reported to be from Homs in Syria; Late Bronze Age; 9 cm high.
Right: standing bronze statuette of a Canaanite 'striking' god, sometimes identified as Reshef; bought in Beirut; Late Bronze Age; 13 cm high.

as Ebla (Tell Mardikh), Mari (Tell Hariri), Alalakh (Tell Atshana) and Ugarit (Ras Shamra) their outstanding reputations. Occasionally clever use of comparisons and analogies may extract illuminating information even from the most basic of ground plans. Ussishkin has done this for the 'southern palace' (no. 1733) at Megiddo. By analogy with the plans of Iron Age palatial buildings in Syria he has interpreted it as a major structure of Solomon's reign.[8] Not only does this extend our understanding of Megiddo at an important period in its history, but it also helps with a better appreciation of the palace Solomon built in Jerusalem, somewhat cryptically described in Kings 7:1–12.

Temples and shrines present many problems of interpretation not easily resolved from their plans and meagre surviving furniture. Even a corpus of religious texts, as at Ugarit, may be related to the daily cult-life of the city temples only in rare instances. Although numerous small statuettes of gods and goddesses survive[9] (Plate 17), and one or two carved stone reliefs depicting deities, they are almost all without identifying inscriptions. In such circumstances links between the names of Canaanite deities known from texts and representations in art must remain tentative in all but a very few cases. Even when an individual temple, such as the Late Bronze Age Fosse Temple at Tell ed-Duweir, is furnished with an unusually rich collection of votive offerings, some even inscribed, the identity of the main deities worshipped there and the nature of the cult is largely a matter of inference. In this case Crowfoot argued[10] that the isolated position of the temple, built over the filled ditch of the earlier city defences, and the absence of architectural features common in large, central city temples, such as a 'Holy of Holies' or a courtyard with open-air altars, pointed to a minor, but popular, cult like that of the divine spirits of vegetation. Similar unorthodox cults may have been the subject of veneration in later Iron Age extra-mural shrines near the Virgin's Spring on Ophel in Jerusalem[11] where figurines were the primary clue. A more confident attribution may be made for the copper miners' shrine at Timna, because of a wealth of appropriate Egyptian votive objects and the known association of the Egyptian goddess Hathor with Semitic miners under Egyptian control in Sinai.[12]

Small Finds

Pottery is the most abundant, the most durable and arguably the most significant of artefacts recovered by excavation on historic sites in Palestine. Petrie was here, as in so much else, the pioneer. 'Pottery is, however, the greatest resource of the archaeologist. For variety of form and texture, for decoration, for rapid change, for its quick fall into oblivion, and for its incomparable abundance, it is in every respect the most important material for study and it constitutes the essential alphabet of archaeology in every land . . . With the brief view of Palestinian pottery gained in a few weeks, on one site at Tell Hesy, I found it possible to ride over mounds of ruins and see the age of them without even dismounting.'[13] If time has rendered us more cautious, it has not seriously impaired the supreme value of this working tool. Petrie was no less confident of the best way to organise such evidence. 'The first necessity for carrying on research either in settlements or cemeteries, is an intimate knowledge of the pottery, and its period, absolute or relative. For this purpose, *a corpus of dated forms is essential*' (my italics).[14]

Although few would deny the wisdom of this approach, especially at the time of writing, it is now regarded as too narrow in its almost exclusive emphasis on changing shape and decoration as indicators of passing time or fresh cultural affinities. It neither exploits fully the cultural significance of ceramic evidence nor approaches it with sufficient attention to the realities of potting. If the technological achievement and economic structure of any

Plate 18   *Above*: Jug of 'Bichrome Ware' from Tell el-Ajjul, Late Bronze Age, I, *c*. 1500 BC.

Plate 19   *Below*: A selection of Late Bronze and Early Iron Age Cypriote pottery vessels (and local copies: second left at rear) from sites in Palestine and Syria.

one period is to be defined, the more that is known of its pottery industries, as providing the commonest and best preserved material evidence, the better. When Albright involved a ceramics expert, J. Palin Thorley, in the study of the potters' techniques at Tell Beit Mirsim Stratum A (Iron Age), he was preparing the way for a new and now increasingly common approach to the study of ancient pottery through the observations of modern professional potters. They are interested primarily in the practical potential of the body material, the combination of clay and tempering, and what it meant for shaping. Franken and his pottery experts have most recently emphasised the relevance of forming techniques as a basis for pottery classification in their studies of the Iron Age pottery from Deir 'Alla and Jericho.[15] It is an important corrective to earlier work, but it can in itself exaggerate a single line of investigation if exclusively used. The Taanach expedition has evolved an equally precise but more balanced approach in which full attention is paid to fabric, form and manufacture.[16] Indeed the advocated technical studies of pottery from excavations are tending to become so complex that their appearance in print is all too likely to be proportionally retarded.

Actual potters' workshops are still rarely discovered and when they are, unless studied by a ceramics expert, do not yield a great deal of information. Cave 4034 at Tell ed-Duweir had been used by potters in the Late Bronze Age. Unbaked sherds and an unbaked figurine, traces of kilns, potter's wheels, pits for preparing the clay for potting, red ochre and a mortar for grinding pigment, shells, pebbles and sherd templates for forming and burnishing vessels were clear indication of their presence.[17] Isolated kilns and potter's wheels are more common than such clear evidence of workshops as this.

Although important observations about pottery have been made through the study of forming methods, more immediately spectacular results have been obtained by the application of scientific techniques of examination to the body of a pot in order to isolate minerals of different origin and, if possible, identify their geological source. These 'chemical fingerprints' may be obtained in a variety of ways, either through analysis by x-ray fluorescence spectrometry or neutron activation, or through the examination of thin sections of pottery under a petrological microscope. This instrument is equipped with optical refinements, which enable the precise determination of mineral and rock inclusions. As clay minerals are too fine-grained to be identified in this way, research is limited to coarse inclusions, either occurring naturally in the clay or added as temper. The types and distribution of these elements are an aid to understanding manufacture as well as the sources of raw material. Wheel turning, for instance, tends to orientate long inclusions parallel to the pot's walls and certain key changes in minerals will

Plate 20   Small burnished pottery juglet in the form of a pomegranate from Jerusalem; later eighth or seventh century BC; for a cosmetic oil or unguent; 8 cm high.

indicate firing temperatures.

A sharp and instructive contrast between old and new approaches to pottery studies is provided by research on 'Bichrome Ware', a distinctive painted pottery of Late Bronze Age I in Palestine (Plate 18). In 1938 Heurtley, in a careful stylistic analysis,[18] concluded that many of the vessels in this style could be attributed to a single master-painter working at Tell el-Ajjul, whence examples of his work had been exported to other parts of Palestine and Cyprus. More recently neutron activation analysis,[19] by Artzy, Perlman and Asaro, has been interpreted as showing that many of the vessels tested came from eastern Cyprus. A distinction was drawn between two families of 'Bichrome Ware', one said to be from Cyprus, and found there at the end of the Middle Bronze Age; and another which is probably local to Megiddo, where it was found in Stratum IX ($\pm$ 1500-1468 BC). Heurtley had noticed a difference but attributed it to a stylistic development in a single cultural setting. The full implications, and validity, of these challenging new results are still to be fully explored.

Although science may steadily improve knowledge of trade in pottery, residues in pots are so rare as seriously to restrict investigation of what was transported in those many vessels that travelled as containers rather than as trade items in their own right. Residues, when tested, are usually of beer, yeast or honey. Jars for transporting wine and vegetable oils are to some extent identified by their form, by stamped handles or by association with special production centres as at el-Jib (Gibeon) (see p. 84). Indirect arguments have sometimes been used to elucidate the original function of traded pottery, as when Merrillees argued that the distinctively shaped Cypriote base-ring juglets of the Late Bronze Age copy the seed head of the opium poppy, and may thus have been used to trade opium in solution.[20]

No review of the role of pottery in archaeological research is complete without a rapid glance at its place in the study of cultural development in the sense defined in chapter 1 (p. 15). Although this is a matter of lesser concern to historic than to prehistoric archaeology, the use of pottery to chart the movements in time and space and the activities of specific peoples, is constant in general studies of Palestinian archaeology. Even if it is appreciated that complex social, economic and political factors contribute to the distribution of pottery, with no coherent relation to the movements and settlements of well defined groups of people, there is enough truth in some 'pots and peoples' equations to make them archaeologically useful as aids to interpretation. So long as it is realised that they are a very blunt instrument constantly in need of sharpening, all is well. They only become more of a hindrance than a help when they are used in complex historical and biblical studies, often by writers unaware of their true archaeological character, to argue for the presence or absence of a particular people on the basis of the presence or absence of the particular ware named after them.

An excellent example of the problems raised by the identifications of particular ceramic styles with certain peoples is presented by 'Philistine pottery' – a distinctive and attractive painted pottery appearing primarily in

Plate 21   Baked clay 'Astarte' plaque and faience face amulet, perhaps of the same
            goddess, from Gezer in Israel; *c*. 1300–1200 BC; 12 and 7 cm high.

the early Iron Age in the region described in the Old Testament as 'Philis-
tia'[21]. It is a hybrid style of pottery owing something to the potters of
Mycenaean Greece, especially in the Argolid, in the forms and designs
painted on it. But local traditions are evident in some shapes, in certain
preferences in the designs, and in the use of red and black paint on a whitish
ground colour. When this pottery first appeared in Palestine in the twelfth
century BC and was later traded from production centres on the coast, the
Philistines were but one of a number of intrusive peoples from the west and
northwest collectively known as the 'Sea Peoples' and listed in Egyptian
inscriptions. Some of these peoples were retained by the Egyptians as mercenaries to garrison cities in coastal Palestine and the Plain of Esdraelon.
When the Egyptians withdrew from Palestine in the later twelfth century,
these mercenaries took power in a number of cities. The distinctive pottery
is certainly closely associated with their activities, but as a group, not as the
Philistines alone, and its presence or absence at any particular site is not
necessarily indicative of the extent of 'Philistine' control.

The methods used to study pottery broadly apply to all other objects of
baked clay, outstanding among them *terracotta statuettes* of human beings

Plate 22   Selection of gold jewellery, including two 'Astarte' pendants and an eight-pointed star, which was her symbol, from Tell el-Ajjul; *c.* 1550 BC; largest pendant 8 cm high.

and animals (Plate 21). These objects, mass produced by hand or in simple moulds, offer the commonest surviving evidence for popular religion and superstition. To establish chronological and geographical distinctions their changing forms, details of their dress and hairstyle, the attributes they sometimes carry, and the contexts in which they have been found, have all been studied. But their precise religious significance more often than not remains elusive. Two caves on the eastern slope of Ophel at Jerusalem, used during Iron Age II, yielded a heterogenous collection of these statuettes, largely women and animals. They seem to have been votive offerings placed

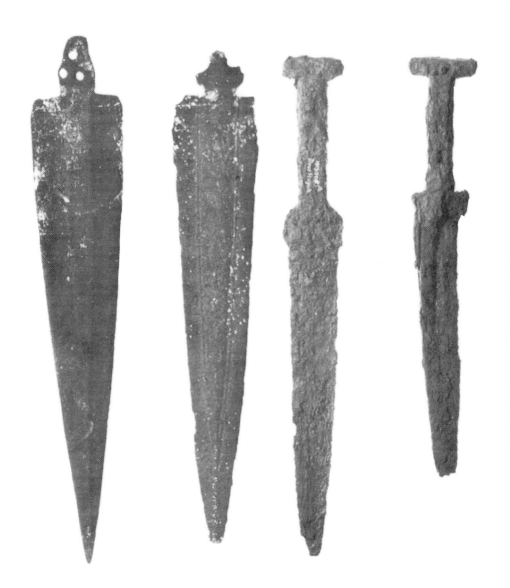

Plate 23 *Left*: Two Middle Bronze Age daggers from Ashdod; among the earliest
weapons made with this alloy of copper and tin in Palestine (formerly T.
E. Lawrence collection); 25 and 19 cm long.

Right: Two iron daggers of a distinctive type (Greek *akinakes*)
introduced into the Levant by Persian troops in the fifth century BC;
from Deve Hüyük, near Jerablus (ancient Carchemish); 34.6 and 29
cm long.

in adjacent shrines for unorthodox cults and deposited in the caves when the shrines were regularly cleared. Even after careful comparative, statistical analysis their exact association with known fertility and solar cults remains an open question.[22]

Precious metals (Plate 22) are so rarely found in Palestinian excavations that they may be set to one side here on the understanding that many of the techniques now used to study *base metal objects* apply equally well to them. The description and typological study of tools, weapons, ornaments and vessels in copper and its alloys, or in iron, have long followed very closely the methods used for pottery. Here again precise description in appropriate metallurgical terminology and detailed examination is increasingly pursued. Metalwork, through rarer than pottery and more subject to recycling in life, to corrosion when buried, is an important aspect of any technology. The range of metal tools and weapons is a useful guide to prevailing agricultural and industrial activities on the one hand, to methods of hunting and warfare on the other. Distinctive new metallurgical techniques or types of artefacts may indicate fresh commercial contacts or intrusive populations, to be traced backwards through earlier examples elsewhere, as with the introduction of iron working at the time of the 'Sea Peoples' in the twelfth century BC. Quality and quantity of metalwork, even in copper and bronze, for which the rare metal tin is required, are a sensitive indicator of prosperity and commercial contacts. Elaborately decorated or luxury metal objects, particularly if they are non-functional, presuppose rich patrons. Less easy to establish, but of the greatest importance, are the origins of the raw materials, the means by which they travelled, and the methods by which they were exploited and used.

Scientific examination of metal objects is crucial if their fabrication methods are to be understood (Plate 24). Viewed under a microscope a specimen taken from a metal object will show the patterns of the crystals that make up the metal and through them whether the metal is pure or an alloy, whether it was cast or wrought, and, if cast, the extent to which it was hot or cold worked after casting. The quality of the metal, its porosity and hardness, will also be evident. Such metallographic studies are a vital complement to the still more common analyses of metal objects to reveal their composition. Such analyses, by spectrographic or other techniques, reveal which artefacts are of unalloyed copper, or arsenical copper, or tin-bronze, and the range of percentage of minor impurities in the metal. These may be classified statistically, grouping metal artefacts into compositional series for comparison with typological classifications.

It has long been hoped that the pattern of minor impurities, or trace

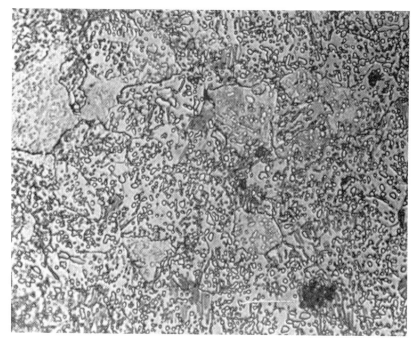

Plate 24 *Above*: Cross-section of an iron dagger blade from Tell el-Fara (south), *c*. 1000–950 BC.

Below: Optical photomicrograph (x 1000) showing the internal structure achieved by forging operations.

Plate 25   Sickle-flints of the later second millennium BC from Tell Jemmeh; traces of plaster with which they were fixed to a wooden handle. Iron sickles gradually replaced flint in Palestine from the tenth century BC; blade about 28 cm long.

elements, in finished objects might be correlated with ore analyses to allow identification of the ores from which the metal had been smelted to make the objects, thus throwing valuable light on the trade in metals. Unfortunately such matching is a complex and unpredictable matter. Even allowing for the technical difficulties of matching composition patterns of ore and object, it would not apply if scrap metal had been used, as it commonly was, at least by the Late Bronze Age. It may only be claimed that such analyses, relatively few of which are yet available for Palestine, give valuable information on alloys and may allow it to be said that the metal of a certain artefact *cannot* be derived from such-and-such an ore deposit. Research continues apace for more reliable 'fingerprints', the isotopes of lead possibly providing one of the potentially most revealing. Isolated pieces of evidence like tin ingots from a Late Bronze Age wreck off Haifa, incised after casting with 'Cypro-Minoan' signs, or a text from Mari, of the Middle Bronze Age, revealing the export of tin westwards to Hazor and Laish (Tell Dan), are for the moment more reliable guides to ancient metal trade.[23]

Of all metal objects *coins* might seem one of the most instructive for archaeologists but coinage did not appear in Palestine until the period of the Persian occupation and then not commonly until the following Hellenistic period. So coins only become useful for archaeological purposes, as in

de Vaux's Qumran excavation,[24] late in the period considered here. Until then such objects as bars, rings and fragments of silver or gold passing by weight were used as currency to replace cumbersome methods of barter. Early references to silver shekels refer to corresponding amounts of silver counted on the basis of the shekel as a unit of weight. The isolated scrap silver hoards which have been found in Palestinian excavations may well have been private 'banks' of such currency.

Analyses of the kind used for pottery fabrics and metal have also begun to aid understanding of the origin, manufacture and distribution of objects made from *faience, frit and glass*[25] (Plate 21). These three closely related artificial substances were used for small objects such as beads, amulets and seals from the fourth millennium BC, and increasingly from about 1600 BC for vessels as well. This later trade was a luxury one with relatively few centres of production, at least outside Egypt, whose wares were widely traded to wealthy patrons. Typological classification and art-historical analysis of patterns have allowed various groups to be identified. Chemical analyses of glazes and body materials, and lead isotope studies for glass, seek to establish more closely centres of production and their repertory of vessels. The term 'faience' is used by archaeologists, misleadingly, to describe an artificial material consisting basically of powdered quartz covered by a vitreous alkaline glaze, varying in colour. Frit is a close relative, often confused with it, also artificially compounded by heating together silica, a copper compound (generally the ore malachite) as a colourant, calcium carbonate and natron (salt). It was widely used as a pigment, often blue in colour. As the chemical composition of ancient glass is essentially that of glaze, its production was an extension of the methods and materials used in faience making.

Stone, and to a lesser extent bone, tools play a large part in prehistoric archaeology, but all too often get overlooked in the richer material cultures of historic times. They remain numerous, if no longer predominant, and no less indicative of a wide range of daily activities. Classification is by form and function as with other small finds, now with increasing attention to the precise geological source of stones and any microscopic evidence for methods of use. The cruder stone objects like loom weights, tethering stones, net sinkers or anchors, door sockets and the like yield most evidence if properly recorded and studied within the context producing them. Weights, by no means always well-shaped or neatly marked with their denomination, are useful evidence for mensuration and commerce. If their identity may be securely established, they may be used to reconstruct the contemporary system of weights, remembering that many communities used independent systems in grocers, jewellers and chemists. The precious and semi-precious stones used for jewellery and seals offer information, more easily investigated through petrology and art historical analysis, on the origin of raw materials and changing fashions. Seals, particularly, with their very varied, handcut designs and occasional inscriptions reveal much about the general level of literacy, about religious imagery and about foreign artistic influences. Bone plays a minor role in continuing to provide cheap and effective personal ornaments, pins and needles, awls and weaving tools, burnishers and scrapers, and digging implements.

There is a whole category of artefacts which are only preserved in Palestine in the most exceptional circumstances. *Wood, rushwork and textiles* have usually survived only in the very dry atmosphere of the Dead Sea Caves or in freak conditions as in the rock cut Middle Bronze Age tombs at Jericho, where even dessicated joints of meat still lay on the original wooden dishes,[26] (Plate 26). These tombs were cut in limestone and then walled up after the burials had been made. Carbon monoxide and methane gas seeping into closed tombs through cracks in the rock replaced the normal air that would have allowed bacteria to live. Consequently organic materials have survived. More commonly, rushwork and woven textiles may only be studied, if at

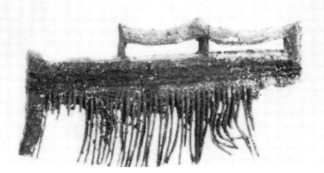

Plate 26 Wooden dish and comb from tombs G.46 and G.73 at Jericho; Middle
Bronze Age; dish 7.5 cm wide.

all, through impressions left on the base of clay pots, which have been stood damp on mats to dry before kiln baking, or textile 'ghosts' left on copper or bronze objects, whose corrosion bears traces of the clothes on which they were laid in a tomb.

It will already be apparent how much the excavator is nowadays dependent on other specialists, by no means all of them natural scientists, for the proper publication of his finds. In one particular area of study, *epigraphy*, this has been true almost from the emergence of archaeological excavation in Palestine. Indeed some of the great pioneers, like the French scholar Charles Clermont-Ganneau (1846–1923), were as much epigraphers as archaeologists. In a region where the documentary tradition, as embodied in the Old Testament, is so pre-eminent any find which throws light on the evolution of scripts and literacy will have a special significance. No native texts of any length have yet been retrieved from Palestine dating before the first millennium BC (Iron Age). The recently discovered archives of Tell Mardik (Ebla) in Syria from the mid-third millennium BC, the fourteenth century tablets from Tell el-Amarna in Egypt, and the predominantly thirteenth century texts from Ras Shamra (Ugarit) in Syria, are the primary points of reference for any reconstructions of Canaanite culture and history through contemporary documents. In the first millennium BC the range of texts revealed by archaeology in Palestine and beyond is very much greater, for then, in West Semitic languages alone, relevant inscriptions have been found in Syria, the Lebanon, Egypt, Iraq, Turkey and the Phoenician and Punic colonies throughout the Mediterranean.

Two important writing systems, much older than anything yet discovered in Palestine, were current there in the historic period for writing various dead languages. The oldest of these, cuneiform ('wedge-shaped') writing, was evolved from about 3500 BC by the Sumerians in southern Iraq, primarily to write on clay.[27] It was adopted in the third millennium BC by the intrusive Semitic Akkadian-speaking peoples to write their own language, that of the peoples known to history as the Babylonians and Assyrians. At much the same time it was also adopted to write local dialects in Syria, as at Ebla. In the second millennium BC Akkadian became the diplomatic language of the Near East and is notably represented by the 'Amarna Letters' and related texts from such sites as Aphek, Gezer, Hazor, Tell el-Hesi, Jericho, Megiddo and Shechem in Palestine.

In the later fourth millennium BC just possibly under Sumerian stimulus, the Egyptians developed a conventionalised picture-symbol script, known from the Greek as hieroglyphic ('sacred carved letters'). As also in Sumer the first signs were pictures of objects, animate and inanimate, directly expressing simple ideas in pictorial terms. But they were rapidly employed in the syllabic spelling of words capable of expressing the many subtleties of speech and thought.[28] For practical everyday purposes the Egyptians developed two cursive scripts, first hieratic (Greek 'priestly' letters) and then demotic (Greek 'popular' letters), a still more cursive variant. Egyptian monumental inscriptions have been found at various places in Palestine, particularly at Megiddo and Bethshan, where at various times they had garrisons. A baked clay bowl from the end of the Late Bronze Age at Lachish bears an Egyptian tax collector's account in the hieratic script (Plate 27).

Both Akkadian (and consequently Sumerian) and ancient Egyptian were deciphered in the nineteenth century, initially through bilingual inscriptions, in which the same text was given in a known and an unknown language. For Akkadian (Babylonian) the key was found in the trilingual rockcut inscription of the Persian king Darius I (c. 522–486 BC) at Behistun in western Iran. It is written in Old Persian, which was partially understood through a surviving sister language Zand, in Elamite, the ancient language of southwest Iran round the ancient city of Susa, and in Akkadian. The first accurate copies and the pioneering decipherment were achieved by the British scholar H. C. Rawlinson (1810–95).[29] For Egyptian the 'Rosetta Stone', now in the British Museum, was the crucial text. It is a copy of a decree issued in 196 BC in Memphis by an assembly of Egyptian priests in honour of King Ptolemy V Epiphanes (c. 203–181 BC), written first in Greek, then in ancient Egyptian, first in hieroglyphic, then in demotic script. It was the French scholar J. F. Champollion (1790–1832), whose profound knowledge of Coptic, the nearest surviving relative to ancient Egyptian, and brilliant analysis of the 'Rosetta Stone' enabled him to formulate the system of grammar and general decipherment upon which modern Egyptology is based.

Both the Akkadian and Egyptian writing systems were complex and cumbersome, with numerous signs. The most significant contribution of the Canaanites to civilization was their invention of a simple script in which less than 30 signs were sufficient to write virtually all human languages. As originally invented the alphabet represented only the consonant sounds of the language for which it was devised. It seems that each letter depicted a specific object whose name began with the particular sound in question. Thus 'b' (Hebrew *bêth;* Greek *bêta*) was denoted by the plan of a house, *bêtu*. This relationship between sign and sound is termed 'acrophonic'. The most significant archaeological evidence for the earliest stages in this development is a series of rock-cut pictographic inscriptions in Sinai. The first discoveries were made in 1905 by Petrie when excavating at Serabit el-Khadem, where in antiquity Semitic workmen had laboured in copper and turquoise mines for the Egyptians. More inscriptions are now known and commonly dated to the sixteenth century BC.

Contemporary with them are a few simple, but very fragmentary and poorly preserved, inscriptions from cities in Palestine, like Gezer and Lachish. They help to confirm the pioneering decipherment of Gardiner in 1917 and the main conclusion of subsequent research by Albright and others that the earliest form of the Canaanite alphabet (ancestral to our own) arose under the direct or indirect influence of Egyptian hieroglyphic, somewhere in Syro-Palestine in the earlier Middle Bronze Age. Its evolution may now be broadly traced through the second millennium BC; but so scarce is archaeological evidence that each new find, however short the inscription, is of unusual importance. Once the alphabetic principle had been discovered its diffusion was relatively rapid.[30]

Tablets found in French excavations under Claude Schaeffer at Ras Shamra (Ugarit) in Syria since 1929 reveal that, under the joint inspiration of the early Canaanite alphabetic system and the Akkadian cuneiform script, scribes there, or elsewhere in the area, had devised an alphabet written not in pictographs, as in the south, but in the simplest possible combination of wedges, apparently uninfluenced by the shape of the pictographs. In this script was written a Canaanite dialect at present known as 'Ugaritic', though there is evidence for its use elsewhere in Syria and Palestine. In a learned journal dated to the very year in which the first tablets were discovered, Charles Virolleaud (1879–1968) made a number of cogent suggestions as to the character of the new script. In 1930 a German scientist Hans Bauer (1878–1937) and Edouard Dhorme (1881–1966), a French cuneiformist and Old Testament scholar, began to decipher it, providing stimulus and information for Virolleaud's classic paper of 1931 in *Syria* in which he gave the right values for nearly all the signs in the Ugaritic alphabet. It was not until 1955, far too late to be of crucial significance, that a tablet was found on which the Ugaritic alphabet was listed with the pronounciation of each letter in terms of Akkadian signs.[31]

By at least the eleventh century BC the main linear alphabetic scripts of the first millennium BC, the Aramaic, the Hebrew and the Phoenician, may be seen emerging from the complex early Canaanite tradition of scripts, though significant archaeological finds from the transitional period are rare and their close dating often difficult. Some are chance finds, not always of known origin, and some are from old excavations where precise recording of locations was ignored. Even those from more recent controlled excavations may not always be precisely dated from the archaeological data, which usually does little more than provide information on the general point in time before or after which they must have been made. Only through a

Plate 27 Two views of a baked clay bowl (restored) from Lachish (Tell ed-Duweir) inscribed in ink in the Egyptian hieratic script with a record of wheat production for harvest taxes (?); end of the Late Bronze Age; 19 cm diameter.

Plate 28   Three modern plaster impressions from eighth and seventh century
stone seals with personal names inscribed on them; the motifs, the four-
winged scarab beetle, the lion and the winged sundisk are all symbols
associated with royal authority.

sequence of such finds may epigraphers plot the evolution of letter shapes
for the various materials, stone, baked clay and papyri, on which they are
usually found, thus steadily creating independent criteria from which to date
inscriptions whose origin is unknown or in doubt.

As the vast majority of 'Early Hebrew' (or palaeo-Hebrew) documents
were probably written on leather or papyrus much has perished and the
witness of archaeology is inevitably very circumscribed.[32] Two main styles
may be defined in the development of the Hebrew script before the later
first millennium BC, both revealed by archaeology in recent times and each
corresponding more or less to well-defined groups of artefacts.[33] A monumental or lapidary script is found on such rare historical inscriptions as that
in the Siloam tunnel as well as on the very much more numerous baked-clay
stamped jar handles (royal and private), inscribed stone weights and seals of
the eighth and seventh centuries BC. A cursive or more practical everyday
script was used for writing in ink on ostraca (pieces of stone, pottery or
bone) as in the famous groups from Samaria of the eighth century BC, and
from Arad and Lachish of the early sixth century BC. Fresh ostraca are
regularly revealed in Iron Age excavations now that it is customary to dip

newly found sherds in water to check carefully for signs of ink before they are passed to the pot-washers whose energetic brushes and muddy water have probably ruined or obscured many ostraca in the past century of excavation. A very rare survivor is a fragmentary letter on papyrus, dated by palaeographic criteria to the eighth century BC, found in the caves of the Wadi Murabba'at.[34] The 'Square Hebrew' script, ancestor of the modern Hebrew alphabet, is not a direct descendant of the palaeo-Hebrew script, but of the Aramaic script of the period of the Persian Empire. It became standardised just before the Christian era and many of the Dead Sea Scrolls are written in it.

Fragmentary *animal bones* found in excavations represent the by-products of many human subsistence and cultural activities which may be inferred by zoologists after careful study. As bones are very rarely found articulated in whole or partial skeletons, archaeological bone evidence presents the zoologist with many problems of identification and analysis. If they were not present at the time of excavation, the director must be able to tell his bone specialists exactly the circumstances in which bones were found and the way in which they were retrieved. Ideally the sample should be as representative as possible. Careful work with a trowel will usually find bones of deer or dog size; but careful sieving with a 5 mm. mesh will be needed to find those of rodents, whilst a mesh of 1.5 mm. will catch the bones of tiny lizards, of fish vertebrae and even the stray rat molar. The introduction of sieving in recent years has yielded not only far greater quantities of tiny and fragmented bone, but also evidence for very small animals that would otherwise be completely overlooked. The source of the bones is crucial to any proper appreciation of significant functional contrasts. Bone debris in living areas, for instance, will tend to consist of the smaller, inconspicuous bone fragments and the smaller animals will predominate, whilst in refuse dumps, larger fragments will be found and larger animals may predominate. All such factors have to be borne in mind when drawing conclusions about daily life from the identified bone counts given in excavation reports.

So far few detailed modern bone reports are available in print from historic sites in Palestine. That for Tell Dan,[35] fortunately, clearly illustrates some of the points already made. In area T at Dan, where the Early Iron Age 'high place' was located, the bones of sheep, goats and cattle indicated that they had been killed off when substantial growth ceased, perhaps representing the rubbish of a population group of high social standing consuming youngish animals. In area B, by contrast, a significant portion of such animals had survived into maturity, indicating an emphasis on secondary products like milk, wool and breeding. This was garbage both from food production and from food consumption, with animals only eaten when they had ceased to be effective producers. Significantly in area B the relative proportions of front to hind limbs was equal, whereas in T the forelimb was 50% more common than the hind, which carries less meat (note a possible connection here with Genesis 32:32–3).

The potential contribution of scientific study of *human bone* is considerably more obvious to the non-specialist and needs no emphasis. No full social reconstruction of any ancient community is complete without examination of the available human bones, normally retrieved from burials. In ideal circumstances these will be undisturbed, articulated skeletons; but often enough the excavator and his bone specialists must deal with disarticulated human bones in tombs used over many generations or with cremations, seeking information where best they may. Evidence of age and sex ratios, of racial or family affinities, of causes of death, of details of diet and disease, as reflected in bone structure, add considerably to any understanding of daily life in specific settlements. Brothwell concluded his pioneering palaeo-pathological study of Middle Bronze Age skeletons from Jericho on a sombre note, 'If these people examined are typical Jerichoans then the standard of health certainly cannot be regarded as high.'[36] He had recognised fractures, long bone osteitis, arthritis and oral diseases.

With modern techniques two categories of *preserved plant remains* can be recovered through excavation: the macroscopic comprising wood, charcoal, seeds and fruit remains, and the microscopic, predominantly pollen. Each presents the botanist with its own problems and will rarely be represented equally well in any one excavation. Wood is most commonly encountered as charcoal. Fortunately the combustion process does not destroy the microscopic structure of the wood. It is therefore possible to identify charcoal almost as readily as uncharred wood, as has been illustrated by work on the Jericho charcoals.[37] With water or chemicals, seeds may be freed from the earth surrounding them on the simple principle that earth sinks whilst they float. Rarer, supplementary information may sometimes be gleaned from grain impressions in pots and from carbonised grains. Whereas wood and pollen can rarely be taken beyond genus, seeds may often be identified to species level. Identification and systematic analysis yields information on food plants, on the character of local flora and vegetation, on the prevailing agricultural routines and on climatic conditions.

In Europe in the last sixty years pollen analysis has transformed the study of ancient man's natural environment. Fluctuations in species of trees, herbs and shrubs have been used to chart how climatically determined forests changed composition through time and how man exploited forested territory.

But pollen is only preserved in soils under certain environmental conditions, which did not, for instance, apply at Jericho. Three soil samples from the tell there failed to yield any pollen.[38] The most favourable conditions for recovering pollen are waterlogged deposits, such as those sampled in recent years from Lake Huleh and the Bay of Haifa in Palestine. The similarity of the results was sufficient to provide a reliable guide to the vegetation and climatic conditions of the region over the last 6000 years.[39]

Pollen grains are remarkable in having walls impregnated with sporopollenin, which can be one of the most bacterially resistant plant materials known. There is also great diversity in the structure of pollen grains, with strong systematic characters, facilitating detailed identifications. Pollen is deposited on all exposed surfaces each year as pollen 'rain' in the flowering season. As it has such wide dispersal, it presents a picture both of vegetation in the collecting area itself and in the surrounding country. The analyst, for accuracy's sake, has to be sure that the pollen from his sampling point is of the same age, that it reflects as far as possible the proportions of the different species represented in the pollen 'rain', and that totally alien material has not been blown in from great distances. As with other aspects of the archaeological record, more than one line of enquiry, say the comparison of seed and pollen analyses, is the most reliable approach to a convincing reconstruction of ancient ecological conditions in any one place or period.

A further line of enquiry, through tree-ring growth (dendrochronology), may only be applied in Palestine in a minor way. It requires old trees with distinct growth rings, which react sensitively to slight climatic fluctuations. Trees and timber suitable for such studies are rare in Palestine. So far such information does not go back much before AD 1000. It suggests only minor climatic fluctuations in that time.

Many of the topics raised by this cursory survey go far beyond the immediate responsibilities of the field archaeologist in presenting his data in print; but they call attention to the necessity for full and accurate publication, within a reasonable time after excavation, as the indispensable basis for all other research. In this archaeologists are notoriously culpable. Numerous excavations, large and small, linger in unpublished limbo, crippling the proper growth of research and compromising any attempts to offer reliable syntheses of available information. For the ultimate goal goes far beyond adequate publication of sections, plans, objects and scientific reports. It seeks no less than a comprehensive understanding of the communities living in Palestine through antiquity. In the period covered by the Old Testament, our main concern in this book, this raises special questions which must be briefly faced in a final chapter.

Notes

1. For example Y. Shiloh, *I.E.J.* 20 (1970), pp. 180–90; G.E. Wright in *Archaeology in the Levant: Essays for Kathleen Kenyon*, Eds. P.R.S. Moorey and P.J. Parr, Warminster, England, 1978, pp. 149–154.
2. O. Tufnell, *Lachish* III, London, 1953, pp. 106–7, fig. 9.
3. W.F. Albright, *The Excavation of Tell Beit Mirsim* III: *The Iron Age* A.A.S.O.R. XXI–II (1943), pp. 60ff.
4. R. Hestrin, *Biblical Archaeologist* 40 (1977), pp. 29ff.
5. de Vaux , *Archaeology and the Dead Sea Scrolls*, London, 1973, pp. 80ff.
6. J.B. Pritchard, *Winery, Defenses and Soundings at Gibeon*, University of Pennsylvania, 1964.
7. Z. Herzog in Y. Aharoni, *Beer-sheba* I, Tel Aviv, 1973, pp. 23–30; for Megiddo, J.B. Pritchard in J.A. Sanders (Ed.), *Essays in Honor of Nelson Glueck, Near Eastern Archaeology in the Twentieth Century*, New York, 1970, pp. 268–76.
8. *Biblical Archaeologist* 36 (1973), pp. 78–105; K.M. Kenyon, *Royal Cities of the Old Testament*, London, 1971.
9. O. Negbi, *Canaanite Gods in Metal*, Tel Aviv, 1976.
10. *Antiquity* XV (1941), pp. 45–9.
11. K.M. Kenyon, *Digging Up Jerusalem*, London, 1974, pp. 139ff.
12. B. Rothenberg, *Timna: Valley of the Biblical Copper Mines*, London, 1972, pp. 125ff.
13. *Methods and Aims*, London, 1904, pp. 16–17.
14. Preface to G. Duncan's *Corpus of Dated Palestinian Pottery*, London 1930; for the standard work see R. Amiran, *Ancient Pottery of the Holy Land*, Jerusalem, 1969.
15. *Excavations at Deir 'Alla* I, Leiden, 1969; *In Search of the Jericho Potters*, Amsterdam, 1974.
16. A.E. Glock, *B.A.S.O.R.* 219 (1975), pp. 9–28.
17. O. Tufnell, *Lachish* IV, London, 1958, pp. 291ff.
18. *Q.D.A.P.* VIII (1939), pp. 21–37.
19. *I.E.J.* 25 (1975), pp. 129–134; *Levant* X (1978), pp. 99–111.
20. *Antiquity* XXXVI (1962), pp. 287–92.
21. N. Sandars, *The Sea Peoples*, London, 1978; another good example is the loose archaeological use of 'Hyksos', cf. Van Seters, *The Hyksos: A New Investigation* (1966).
22. T.A. Holland, *Levant* IX (1977), pp. 121–155.
23. J.D. Muhly, *Copper and Tin*, New Haven, Connecticut, 1973.
24. de Vaux, op.cit., passim.
25. E. Peltenburg, *World Archaeology* 3 (1971), pp. 6–12.
26. S. Dorrell in K.M. Kenyon, *Jericho* II, London, 1965, pp. 704–7.
27. G.R. Driver, *Semitic Writing : from pictograph to alphabet*, 3rd. edition, Oxford, 1976, chap. 1.
28. A. Gardiner, *Egyptian Grammar*, 3rd. edition, Oxford, 1957.
29. C.H. Gordon, *Forgotten Scripts : the story of their decipherment*, London, 1968; M.W.M. Pope, *The Story of Decipherment : from Egyptian hieroglyphic to Linear B*, London, 1975.
30. F.M. Cross, 'The Origin and Early Evolution of the Alphabet', in *Eretz Israel*

8 (1967), pp. 8*–24*; P. Kyle McCarter, *The Antiquity of the Greek Alphabet and the Early Phoenician Scripts*, London, 1975.
31. G.R. Driver, op.cit., pp. 148ff.
32. A.R. Millard, 'The Practice of Writing in Ancient Israel', *Bib. Arch.* 35(1972), pp. 98–111.
33. D. Diringer, *The Alphabet : A Key to the History of Mankind*, London, 1968, chaps. 14–15.
34. P. Benoit *et al.*, *Discoveries in the Judaean Desert* II, Oxford, 1961, pp. 93ff.
35. P. Wapnish *et al.* *B.A.S.O.R.* 227 (1977), pp. 35–62.
36. K.M. Kenyon, *Jericho* II, p. 692
37. A.C. Western, *Levant* III (1971), pp. 31–40.
38. Op.cit., p. 32.
39. A. Horowitz, *Paléorient* 2(2) (1974), pp. 407–414.

Recommended Reading

In this chapter much bibliographical information has been intentionally worked into the footnotes.

An enormous amount of information from archaeological sources is referred to in entries in, *The Interpreter's Dictionary of the Bible*, Nashville and New York, 1962, with the *Supplementary Volume*, 1975.

For the impact of science, the following books are a general guide, though they have virtually no illustrative material from Palestine,
M.J. Aitken, *Physics and Archaeology*, 2nd Edition, Oxford, 1974.
D. Brothwell *et al.* (Ed.), *Science in Archaeology* London, revised edition, 1969.
G.W. Dimbleby, *Ecology and Archaeology*, The Institute of Biology's Studies in Biology, no. 77, London, 1977.
M.S. Tite, *Methods of Physical Examination in Archaeology*, London, 1972.

For a combination of field research and experiment in archaeology see,
B. Rothenberg *et al.*, *Chalcolithic Copper Smelting*, Archaeo-Metallurgy I, Institute for Archaeometallurgical Studies, London, 1978. This is based on study of the Timna region in Israel.

7

After Excavation:
The use and abuse of archaeology in biblical studies

> If the results of archaeology seem to be opposed to the conclusions of text criticism, the reason may perhaps be that not enough archaeological facts are known or that they have not been firmly established; the reason also may be that the text has been wrongly interpreted. (de Vaux in J. A. Sanders (ed.), *Glueck Festschrift*, New York 1970, p. 78.)

The contribution of archaeology to biblical studies, if often controversial, has been fundamental. Since the middle of the nineteenth century peoples and languages only obliquely known from the Bible have been regularly rediscovered through excavations in the Near East. Archaeology in Syria and Iraq has revealed archives of tablets illustrating every aspect of the Assyro-Babylonian civilisation which played so crucial a role in many biblical narratives. The discovery above all of lost Babylonian and Ugaritic literature, offered numerous points of comparison with the Old Testament in form and content. In Palestine itself finds of papyri, outstandingly the Dead Sea Scrolls, ostraca and other inscriptions have been no less fundamental to modern thinking on numerous biblical problems. This flow of information from extra-biblical texts has been eagerly received by biblical scholars, critically assessed and more or less readily assimilated into the general body of knowledge.

The relationship of biblical scholarship and text-free, or more specifically 'dirt', archaeology has on the whole been less happy. Whereas biblical scholars, trained in the arts of textual criticism and analysis, have naturally applied them to the documents revealed by archaeology, some have been less ready to apply equally rigorous and equally appropriate standards to the evidence provided by archaeological stratigraphy and typology. At the same time some archaeologists, either unprepared to accept the most authoritative modern interpretations of the biblical text, or too eager to establish the priority of their own discoveries or the truth of some sectarian beliefs, have made extravagant or unwarranted claims easily exposed as facile or fallacious by more sober biblical scholarship.

The previous chapters have sought to show something of the special character of archaeological evidence and its potential for reconstructing the culture and daily life of ancient Palestine in the period covered by the Old Testament. Archaeological evidence is like that provided by any witness. It may speak with many tongues; it is extremely partial; and more often than not it may seem to be deceptively eager to give the anticipated answer. It must be sharply cross-examined at all times by interrogators constantly alive to the special character of this particular witness and the type of evidence it is best able to provide. If it is asked archaeologically nonsensical questions, it will give nonsensical answers. To establish this distinction rapidly some clear idea of the differences between the kind of evidence a historian controls and that within the range of an archaeologist, not provided with relevant textual material in his excavations, is essential. To do this concisely it will be necessary to categorise history in rather a crude, restricted way, in order to highlight the special character of archaeological information.

History is much concerned with events, archaeology almost exclusively with the background against which events take place. The short term interplay of cause and effect in human affairs constitutes a significant part of history's subject matter. This is not so in archaeology, whose raw material is most readily interpreted in terms of the broad economic, social and technological factors affecting human life. Archaeologists in Palestine, as elsewhere, certainly uncover direct evidence of events, usually of the catastrophic kind, such as earthquakes and burnings of cities by enemies. But the extent to which they may be reconstructed from archaeological evidence alone is highly circumscribed. The details upon which the precision of historical reconstruction rests are supplied only by written sources. The most decisive events in world history have left no immediate trace whatsoever in the archaeological record. It has been said, with some justification, that 'the archaeologist would be totally unaware of any important ethnic changes at the end of the Late Bronze Age were it not for the biblical tradition.'[1]

This crucial restriction, which is often overlooked in the more elaborate forms of biblical archaeology, may best be illustrated from a rare, if not unique, case in Palestine where historical and archaeological evidence of an unusually precise kind appear together. Yadin's excavations at Masada in 1963–5 revealed traces of a major conflagration across the site at the end of its main occupation. A *terminus post quem* for this fire, not it may be noted a precise date, was provided by coins: shekels representing all the years of the First Jewish Revolt, from the issues for year one to the very rare issues for year five (AD 70). They, and inscriptions on stone and papyri identified the defenders as Jewish; information endorsed by such specialist structures as the ritual baths, a synagogue and what may be a *beth midrash* (school). Beyond that the archaeological evidence alone does not take us. A

Plate 29   Et-Tell, usually identified as ancient Ai.

circumvallation, camps and a massive siege ramp reveal in their distinctive layout the presence of Romans as the eventually triumphant foe. Without the dramatic account of this siege surviving in the writings of the historian Josephus (AD 37–c.100), it would have been impossible to reconstruct in detail the final events of the siege and give their exact date (AD 74). Indeed the excavator made the point very well himself by reprinting the ancient historian's vivid narrative in his own lively popular account of the excavations.[2]

Commonly the historian is concerned with comparatively short periods of time, often even just fractions of a single human life-span. The archaeologist, in very marked contrast, is rarely dealing with evidence that may be meaningfully treated in terms of a single human life. Even with the help of the most modern scientific methods of absolute date determination (see

pp. 72ff), the archaeologist is unable to pin down a specific destruction level, for instance, within much less than the span of a generation unless he has sound ancillary evidence, drawn from a written source, for associating it with a particular campaign. Even if it were possible to date the great destruction level at Tell ed-Duweir (Lachish) at the end of the Bronze Age, where bronze fragments bearing a cartouche of Ramses III now provide a *terminus post quem*, the victors could not confidently be named from the archaeological evidence alone.[3] It is then a very relative matter when archaeologists speak of 'contemporary' destructions. If their evidence is entirely that of artefacts, wholly unaided by texts, 'contemporary' might well range over decades. Consequently, archaeological data is most satisfactorily handled in terms of the life of a total human community, preferably over an extended period of time.

This time dimension has an important social complement with implications not always evident in over-enthusiastic accounts of the role archaeology might play in Old Testament study. The historian is regularly able to deal with those notable individuals whose activities most commonly leave their mark in the written record. The textless archaeologist has no such access to the individuals of the past, its great men or heroes. He deals with the submerged majority in any social system or with the ruling minority as a group or class, not as a series of identifiable personalities. If we remember that such men as David and Solomon have yet to be identified in a contemporary or near contemporary extra-biblical inscription, we appreciate more readily the fallacy of looking to dirt archaeology for precise information on such figures as Abraham, Moses or Joshua, whether or not we accept them as historical. Only a very meticulous study of a whole range of archaeological information, and rigorous analysis of the negative as much as the positive evidence, allows any kind of valid conclusions to be drawn about possible archaeological settings for events recorded in Genesis and Exodus or Joshua and Judges. Questions framed about specific individuals, say Hammurabi of Babylon or Sennacherib of Assyria, or particular events, like the fall of Jerusalem to Nebuchadnezzar, may be appropriate even for historians studying the most primitive written sources relevant to them or their time, but never for archaeologists wholly without written records.[4]

To crystallise these vital distinctions round instances where the biblical text and related archaeological evidence appear to be at odds is not difficult. Two examples are particularly instructive for the sharp way in which they polarise approaches: the excavations at et-Tell (Plate 29), commonly identified as ancient Ai, and at Jericho, in relation to the Joshua narratives. Since extreme cases are often the best for revealing the heart of a problem, the archaeology of these two sites, classic cruxes in biblical archaeology, will be taken as the primary illustrations. Both present complex problems, much discussed and still unresolved,[5] which cannot be entered into here, where I wish only to lay emphasis on the role of the archaeological data in the debate. In one important respect the two sites differ. Whereas it has never been cogently argued that Tell es-Sultan is not the site of ancient Jericho, the identification of modern et-Tell with Ai has been challenged forcefully on a number of occasions and the equation may not yet be taken as beyond reasonable doubt. If the reader rejects this identification, then the problems presented by the excavations at et-Tell disappear with it, at least for the moment. Only when excavations have been undertaken at all sites suggested as alternatives for ancient Ai and Bethel (the question of their location is interrelated) will it be possible to assess this issue properly.

Accepting for the sake of demonstration that Ai was at et-Tell, as many

Plate 30   Et-Tell: view of the early Iron Age settlement.

scholars still do, the relevant archaeological evidence may be simply set out. It was excavated briefly by Garstang in 1928, by Judith Marquet-Kraus in 1933–5 and by Callaway in 1964–70. It was an outstanding example of an urban settlement during the earlier third millennium BC, violently destroyed about 2300 BC and then unoccupied for centuries. It was re-occupied early in the Iron Age, when an unwalled village was established on the old mound by people then moving into the area, creating settlements in new places of strategic importance or on old abandoned sites (Plate 30). Their settlement at et-Tell was characterised by use of a collared-rim storage jar common to all the earliest Iron Age sites in this region. The site was again deserted before burnished pottery became a regular component of Iron Age pottery production, sometime in the early or mid-eleventh century BC. The date of the first establishment of this village in the twelfth century BC may not be closely fixed with the available ceramic evidence; nor may the identity of the new settlers be confidently established from the archaeological data. Thus there is no archaeological evidence for a military sack of the settlement at et-Tell between about 2500 BC and the mid-eleventh century, and even then the evidence for an assault of any kind is negligible.

A negative conclusion is hard to avoid except through some form of special pleading, independent of the archaeological discoveries at et-Tell, like Albright's theory that events at Beitîn were erroneously placed at Ai. Joshua 8:28 is explicit, 'So Joshua burnt Ai to the ground, and left it the destitute ruined mound it remains to this day.' Joshua 7–8 appears to describe a fortified city: a gate is specifically mentioned, and the military tactics seem to imply something more than an unfortified village. If et-Tell is ancient Ai, the archaeological evidence at present available best sustains the view that this particular passage is not historically sound: that the Ai destruction narrative is a legend, perhaps an aetiological story to explain the deserted mound. Even if the Conquest is dated much earlier or later than the thirteenth century context now generally argued, excavations at et-Tell do not provide any indication of a fortified town burnt to the ground.

The case of Jericho is more complex, as the information provided by archaeology is less precise. Two preliminary points must be made. The top of the mound at Jericho (Tell es-Sultan) has undoubtedly been much eroded. It has consequently been argued that whole periods of occupation could have been obliterated. Such indeed might be the case; but it is axiomatic in field archaeology that any such occupations, had they existed, would have left some trace, if no more than sherds of characteristic pottery, down the slopes of the mound or on its periphery. If there are no such sherds and no extra-mural graves, then any occupation of that particular period on the original mound summit is highly unlikely. Secondly, modern knowledge of the time range of occupation on the *tell* during the critical period, the Late Bronze Age, turns exclusively on ceramic criteria which by their very nature are imprecise.

Tell es-Sultan (Plate 3) was first excavated by the Palestine Exploration Fund in 1873, then by Sellin in 1907–9, by Garstang from 1930–6 and by Kathleen Kenyon from 1952–8. Her conclusions radically modified those of her predecessor, particularly in relation to the question of Late Bronze Age occupation. The last phase of the Middle Bronze Age town was violently destroyed by fire sometime in the sixteenth century BC on present dating. Only very scanty remains have been found of the settlement built on the rain-washed debris of this burnt town, which Kathleen Kenyon believed had been deserted throughout the fifteenth century BC. These included Garstang's 'Middle Building' and his 'Palace' (which may indeed be Iron Age), but significantly not the double city wall he had attributed to this period; it was much earlier. Kathleen Kenyon found only fragments of a house wall and floor-level of the Late Bronze Age occupation. On the evidence of meagre pottery finds, and she only found one Late Bronze Age pot *in situ* in a structure, in 1957 she dated this period of occupation to the third quarter of the fourteenth century BC; in 1976 she preferred to say that 'the site was re-occupied soon after 1400 BC and abandoned in the second half of the fourteenth century.' This dating is broadly confirmed by pottery from five Middle Bronze Age tombs, excavated by Garstang off the *tell*, which had been re-used in the Late Bronze Age. The absence of Egyptian royal scarabs later than Amenophis III, and of Jericho from the 'Amarna Letters', might be taken to indicate a *floruit* for this settlement before mid-century. Neither Garstang nor Kenyon found clear archaeological evidence for the ninth century settlement of Hiel the Bethelite (1 Kings 16:34); but they did reveal occupation on the flanks of the mound, in successive building levels and one massive structure dating from Iron Age I-IIc.

Here, as at et-Tell/Ai, the negative archaeological evidence bearing on the historicity of the Joshua conquest narratives is considerable. The only real options it leaves for those who wish to argue for historicity is to associate Joshua's attack with the end of the Middle Bronze Age city, as Bimson has recently done (but that opens up a whole fresh range of archaeological problems) or advance it well into Iron Age I.[6]

By isolating Ai and Jericho in this way, if only for the sake of demonstration, the reader has been drawn into a basic methodological error. It is in the general picture, not in the particular and possibly exceptional, that the archaeological evidence is seen to offer its proper witness. The transition from the Late Bronze Age to the Early Iron Age (or from the Middle to the Late Bronze Age if that is the chosen context) must be studied in archaeological terms through a careful examination of the overall settlement pattern. Existing areas of settlement will then be contrasted with regions recently penetrated. Careful attention will need to be paid to sites in established settlement areas showing evidence for destruction at this time. Particular interest will attach to the correlation of such destructions across time and the fate of each site, to show whether it was rapidly re-occupied, and if so whether by newcomers, or whether it was abandoned, either briefly or permanently. Supplementary examinations of artefacts, notably pottery, will seek to reveal whether craft traditions persisted through breaks in occupation or if new trends had come in. If they did, their place in the newly settled areas and their ultimate geographical origins will help in identifying the source of newcomers. Only with a clear and carefully organised review of all the archaeological evidence over a substantial period of time is the archaeologist in a position to confront the textual tradition. Even then it must be constantly recalled that the information each provides is different in kind and that a single closely dated find, like the cartouche of Ramses III from

Tell ed-Duweir (p. 113), may completely modify archaeological chronologies based on pottery alone.

If the use of archaeological evidence to test the historicity of biblical narratives involves methodological questions extending at times dangerously far from material over which the archaeologist has first hand control, no such problem faces its relevance to the material culture portrayed in the Old Testament. Here like is matched with like; surviving remains may be directly mustered to illuminate ancient descriptions and assist with translation of obscure technical terms. Modern study of Solomon's Temple serves as an oustanding instance of this.

In 1 Kings 6–7 the Temple and its furnishings are described in a literary manner, not with the coherence and detail of an architectural blueprint, though technical terms are involved.[7] In view of the history of the site on which it stood it is highly unlikely that any of this building has survived. We may only hope to reconstruct it on paper and then with initial drawbacks, for the description does not give certain vital details and is obscure about others. Even if no final reconstruction is now possible, much archaeological evidence may still be mustered to throw light on the building in its original form.

One initial point is crucial for anyone seeking the best archaeological parallels. The Old Testament makes clear that the men who cut the timber and shipped it, the carpenters and the stonemasons, certainly the master smith, Hiram, and possibly the master mason, were all Phoenicians among whom Canaanite culture was a living tradition. The three-fold division of Solomon's Temple into *Ulam* ('porch'), *Hekal* ('Holy Place') and *Debir* ('Holy of Holies') is common in Late Bronze Age Canaanite temples, as for instance at Hazor, and in Iron Age Syria, as at Tell Tainat. In the latter city temple and palace were also closely associated as at Jerusalem. A shrine in the Iron Age fortress at Tell Arad, subsequent to the time of Solomon, in some ways resembles the biblical description of Solomon's Temple; but whether it was indeed a 'House of Yahweh' or some lesser place of worship is still debated. In some of these temples, as at Jerusalem, walls on stone footings were locked together with a timber framework and faced with woodwork. The two pillars which stood before the porch, not as part of its structure, may be seen on small model temples of the period from Cyprus and Palestine, and such pillars are mentioned in classical descriptions of Phoenician shrines. Their precise significance is uncertain. They may well have been the time-honoured Canaanite *maṣṣboth*, though there is no agreed interpretation of their recorded names, *Yakin* and *Bo'az*.

It is the minor arts of the Phoenicians that offer the best surviving clues to the Temple's interior decoration. Here the wooden panels of the walls

Plate 31   Ivory plaque in the Phoenician style from an Assyrian royal palace at Nimrud in Iraq, eighth century BC. Such sphinxes may be the biblical cherubim. 9 cm long.

and doors were carved with cherubim, palm trees, gourds and other flowers. The Phoenicians produced a very distinctive range of carved ivory plaques for inlaying into wooden furniture. Examples have been found at Samaria and sites in Syria, but it is those from royal palaces at Nimrud in Assyria that offer the widest range of evidence. Like the carved ivories of the Canaanites in the Late Bronze Age they owed much to Egyptian inspiration, though the Egyptian themes and motifs were more often than not used in a non-Egyptian manner. Floral patterns and monsters are prominent in these inlays. One of their most characteristic designs included creatures with winged leonine bodies and human heads, almost certainly to be identified with the biblical cherubim (Plate 31). Wooden images of such creatures, plated with gold, formed the throne of Yahweh within the 'Holy of Holies' with the tablets in the Ark of the Covenant, a gold plated wooden chest, set at its feet as if to form a footstool. Such chairs or thrones, their sides and backs formed of winged creatures, part beast, part human, had long formed part of royal furnishings in Canaan, where they are shown on ivories, as at Megiddo. In a Canaanite temple the image of deity would have sat on the throne; but in Solomon's Temple this was, of course, proscribed and only the invisible Yahweh was held to be present.

The mobile furniture of the temple, the altars and incense burners, may be evoked by less ornamental, smaller, examples from a number of shrines both in Late Bronze Age Canaan and Iron Age Israel. Many of them have the characteristic vertical projection, or horn, at each of the top corners. The ten wheeled trolleys in the main courtyard are directly paralleled by bronze models from Cyprus and Megiddo, often with decorations in the panels and frames as on their biblical counterparts (1 Kings 7:29). The enormous bronze basin ('sea') borne on the backs of bulls has to be reconstructed from more diverse sources in Cyprus and the Near East; but it is entirely consonant with what is known of contemporary craftsmanship and iconography.

A single case will serve to show how directly archaeological evidence may provide the clue to obscure technical vocabulary. In a number of places the Old Testament refers to *ḥammanîm* (Lev. 26:30; 2 Chron. 14:4;34:4,7; Ezek. 6:4,6). The *ḥammān*, an object set up in high places alongside altars to Baal, was always condemned to be burnt or broken up when the cult furniture of pagan worship was execrated. A stone altar brought to Europe from Palmyra in 1751 (Plate 33, figure 5), and now in Oxford, bears the inscription, 'In the month of September of the year 396 (AD 85) Lišamš and Zebîdā made and offered this *ḥammān* and this altar to Samaš, the god of the house of their father.'[8] The stone altar is clearly the surviving inscribed stone – but what of the *ḥammān*? Happily the front of the altar bears a relief showing Lišamš and Zebîdā standing on either side of an incense burner, with the flames in which the grains of incense were cast clearly depicted. This then is the *ḥammān*, probably in this instance of metal, which had once stood on the stone base inscribed and carved at the donor's order. All such references in the Old Testament would thus appear to be describing perfume-braziers, though they need not always, if ever, have been precisely like this Palmyrene example.

Where text and monument are brought into such direct contact is a good point to end, if only because there the problems of methodology are refreshingly minimal. The art of distinguishing proper from improper searches for biblical connections in the archaeological record may only be acquired

Plate 32 Tiny ivory bull support for a small tray or dish; found at Nimrud in
Assyria, though probably made in Syria in the eighth century BC; such
miniature supports are reminiscent of the monumental bronze 'oxen'
supporting Solomon's great 'sea' (1 Kings 7:25); 7.3 cm long.

through reading far wider than such a brief book as this can provide. Indeed
the line is so hard to draw with confidence that no one approach carries full
conviction. All an introductory essay may hope to do is to set out as clearly
as possible the grounds for asserting two primary, if constantly neglected,
points about that complex region where the 'archaeology of Palestine' and
'biblical archaeology' overlap. First, the archaeology of Palestine in the
Bronze and Early Iron Ages is no different in kind from that of any other
part of the world, save in the survival of an unusually rich range of ancillary
written sources. It may only be studied in the 1980s through those methods
and concepts, appropriate to it as an independent discipline, which are
equally applicable anywhere in the world where man has been. Secondly, if
archaeological data is uncritically and selectively approached with biblical
concepts in mind, it will, not surprisingly, seem to confirm the particular
viewpoints they represent. Archaeological information proves nothing about
the biblical tradition, it only offers fresh matter in the weighing of proba-
bilities. It is, of necessity, circumstantial evidence and will only deceive if
it be taken for that of eye-witnesses.

Plate 33 Stone altar, dated AD 85 from Palmyra, showing an incense altar
(*ḥammān*); 48 cm high.

Figure 5   Drawing of the figures and the incense altar on an altar from Palmyra,
dated AD 85 (cf. plate 33).

1. H. Franken, *Cambridge Ancient History* II(2) (1975), p. 332.
2. Y. Yadin, *Masada*, London, 1966, pp. 232ff.
3. Unpublished, 1978.
4. For a good illustration of the use of textual and archaeological evidence to resolve a historical problem see N.Na'aman, 'Sennacherib's campaign to Judah and the date of the *lmlk* stamps', *Vetus Testamentum* XXX (1979), pp. 61ff.
5. For an up-to-date archaeological summary and bibliography of both sites see *Encyclopaedia of Archaeological Excavations in the Holy Land*; for Ai, particularly, see recently J. Maxwell Miller, 'Archaeology and the Israelite Conquest of Canaan : Some Methodological Observations', *P.E.Q.* (1977), pp. 87ff.; for Jericho recently J.J. Bimson, *Dating Exodus and Conquest*, Sheffield, 1978, pp. 115 ff.; for Bethel (located at Beitun) see J.L. Kelso, *The Excavations of Bethel (1934-60) A.A.S.O.R.* 39, (1968); this report is seriously compromised by overt 'biblical archaeology', cf. W.G. Dever, (Archaeological Methods and Results : A Review of Two Recent Publications', *Orientalia* 40 (1971), pp. 459ff.
6. Bimson, op.cit., passim; his archaeological interpretation and dating of the final phase of the Middle Bronze Age are in themselves debatable.
7. For an exhaustive account see Th. A. Busink, *Der Tempel von Jerusalem von Salomo bis Herodes*, Leiden, 1970; more simply G.E. Wright, *Biblical Archaeology*, London, 1957, pp. 136ff.
8. H. Ingholt in *Mélanges Syriens offerts à M. Réné Dussaud* II, Paris, 1939, pp. 795ff.

Recommended Reading

1. General

Y. Aharoni, *The Archaeology of the Land of Israel*, London, 1982.
Y. Aharoni, *The Land of the Bible*, 2nd revised edition, London, 1979.
K.M. Kenyon, *Archaeology in the Holy Land*, 4th edition, 1979.
J. Murphy O'Connor, *The Holy Land: an archaeological guide from earliest times to 1700*, Oxford, 1980.

2. With reference to the Old Testament

J. Aviram (Ed.), *Biblical Archaeology Today*, Jerusalem 1982.
H.J. Franken, *A Primer of Old Testament Archaeology*, Leiden, 1963.
H.D. Lance, *The Old Testament and the Archaeologist*, London, 1983.
K.M. Kenyon, *The Bible and Recent Archaeology*, revised edition by P.R.S. Moorey, London, 1987.
D. Winton Thomas (Ed.), *Archaeology and Old Testament Study*, Oxford, 1967.

3. Specific Sites

(a) *General accounts*
N. Avigad, *Discovering Jerusalem*, Oxford, 1980.
J.R. Bartlett, *Jericho*, Cambridge, 1982.
A. Curtis, *Ugarit (Ras Shamra)*, Cambridge, 1985.

S. Dalley, *Mari and Karana: Two Old Babylonian Cities*, London, 1984.

G.I. Davies, *Megiddo*, Cambridge, 1986.

K.M. Kenyon, *Digging up Jericho*, London, 1965.

K.M. Kenyon, *Digging up Jerusalem*, London, 1974.

K.M. Kenyon, *Royal Cities of the Old Testament*, London, 1971.

J.B. Pritchard, *Gibeon, Where the Sun stood Still*, Princeton, 1962.

B. Rothenberg, *Timna: Valley of the Biblical Copper Mines*, London, 1972.

R. de Vaux, *Archaeology and the Dead Sea Scrolls*, London, 1973.

G.E. Wright, *Shechem, the biography of a biblical city*, London, 1965.

Y. Yadin, *Hazor: the rediscovery of a great citadel of the Bible*, London, 1975.

Y. Yadin, *Masada: Herod's fortress and the Zealot's last stand*, London, 1966.

(b) *Excavation Reports*

The layman wishing to read his way into basic excavation reports is best advised to start with the most explicit and clearly organised, such as,

W.F. Albright, *The Excavation of Tell Beit Mirsim II, The Bronze Age*, A.A.-.S.O.R. 17 (1938).

W.F. Albright, *The Excavation of Tell Beit Mirsim III, The Iron Age*, A.A.-.S.O.R. 21–22. (1943).

J.W. Crowfoot *et al.*, *Samaria-Sebaste I–III*, London, 1942–57.

K.M. Kenyon, *Jericho* I–II, London, 1960, 1965.

K. Torzcyner, *Lachish, I: The Lachish Letters*, London, 1938.

O. Tufnell, *et al.*, *Lachish* II–IV, London, 1940, 1953, 1958.

Once acquainted with the form of such reports he will then be prepared to read as he wishes, guided by E.K. Vogel, *Bibliography of Holy Land Sites*, H.U.C. Cincinnati, 1971; part II (1970–81), Cincinnati, 1982, or bibliographies in the *Encyclopedia of Archaeological Excavations in the Holy Land* (see p. 54 here).

4. History

J. Bright, *A History of Israel*, 3rd edition, London, 1981.

G. Garbini, *History and Ideology in Ancient Israel*, London, 1988.

J.H. Hayes and J. Maxwell Miller, *Israelite and Judaean History*, London, 1977.

J.A. Soggin, *A History of Israel: from the beginnings to the Bar Kochba Revolt A.D. 135*, London, 1984.

R. de Vaux, *The Early History of Israel: to the Period of the Judges*, London, 1976.

Indexes

Names

Abraham 114
Adam Smith, G. 36
Africanus 72
Aharoni, Y. 32
Albright, W. F. 16, 26, 27, 45, 69, 76, 79, 83, 88, 102, 116
Alexander the Great 74
Alkios 37
Amenophis I 74
Ammisaduqa 76
Ashur-Dan 76

Baal 21, 120
Bauer, H. 102
Bliss, F. J. 24, 25, 39, 72
Burdett-Coutts, A. 22

Callaway, J. 79, 115
Champollion, J. F. 101
Childe, G. 15
Clermont-Ganneau, C. 37, 100
Crowfoot, J. W. 28, 86

Darius I 101
Darwin, C. 13, 68
David, King 114
de Vaux, R. 71–2, 84, 97, 110
Dever, W. 50–52
Dhorme, E. 102
Djer 80
Dunayevsky, M. 32

Eusebius 72

Fabri, G. 21
Falke, O. 33
Fisher, C. S. 26
Franken, H. 88
Frere, J. 11

Gardiner, A. 102
Garstang, J. 48–9, 115, 116–117
Glueck, N. 32, 33, 40, 43, 45
Guy, P. L. O. 40

Hammurabi 76
Hathor 53, 86
Helena, Empress 20

Heurtley, W. A. 89–90
Hiel, the Bethelite 117
Huxley, T. H. 13

Josephus 71, 72, 112
Joshua 48, 114

Kenyon, K. M. 16, 28, 30, 48, 69, 116–117

Lapp, P. 52
Libby, W. F. 77–8
Lyell, C. 68

Macalister, R. A. S. 24, 25, 51–2
Manetho 72, 73
Mardokempados (Marduk-apla-iddina) 74
Marquet-Kraus, J. 115
Merrillees, R. 90
Morlot, A. 15
Moses 114

Nebuchadnezzar II 40, 114
Nabonassar 74

Omri 28

Petrie, W. M. F. 24, 26, 32, 38, 46, 48, 72, 101
Piggott, S. 16, 18
Poidebard, A 33
Pritchard, J. B. 84
Ptolemy 74
Ptolemy V Epiphanes 101

Ramses II 73
Ramses III 113, 117
Rawlinson, H. C. 101
Reisner, G. 25, 26, 28
Renan, E. 21
Robinson, E. 20, 21, 38
Rothenberg, B. 52

Schaeffer, C. F. A. 70, 102
Schliemann, H. 24
Sellin, E. 116
Sennacherib 60, 114
Sesostris III 74
Shamshi-Adad I 76

Places

Sinmagir 77
Smith, E. 20
Solomon, King 50, 53, 84, 85, 114, 118–120
Syncellus 72

Theon 74–6
Thorley, J. P. 88
Tufnell, O. 60

Ussher, Archbishop 68
Ussishkin, D. 85

Vespasian 68
Virolleaud, C. 102

Warren, C. 21
Wheeler, R. E. M. 6, 28
Wiegand, Th. 33
Wilson, C. 22
Wood, R. 20
Woolley, C. L. 43
Wright, G. E. 30

Yadin, Y. 32, 48–50, 111

Zimrida 39

Abydos 73
Acre 21
Ai (et-Tell) 30, 80, 114–117
ʿAin Feshka 84
Alalakh (Atshana) 85
Alexandria 74
Ammon 33
Aphek 100
Arad 32, 60, 80, 104, 118
Azekah 40

Baalbek 20
Bab edh-Draʿ 52
Babylon 74
Banias 23
Beersheba 23, 32, 42, 60, 84
Behistun 101
Beirut 21
Bethel (Beitin) 114, 116
Bethshan 80, 101
Byblos 21

Cape Gelidonya 33
Cyprus 90, 120

Dead Sea 42, 52, 71, 84, 98, 105
Deir ʿAlla 69, 88
Denmark 12
Dhahr Mirzbaneh 52
Dibon (Dhiban) 37

Ebla (Tell Mardikh) 85, 100
Edom 33
Eglon 24, 38–40
Egypt 72–4, 97, 100
el-Jib (Gibeon) 37, 84
er-Riha 37
Esdraelon 91
Europe 106

Gaza 24
Gezer 24, 25, 30, 37, 40, 48–52, 100, 102
Gibeon (el-Jib) 37, 40
Gilead 33
Gilgal 36
Greece 91

Haifa 96, 107

127